W9-AWF-626

The Key to Self-Awareness in the Birth Chart

Ever wonder why do you do the things you do? Through the Midheaven (tenth-house cusp), you can pinpoint the psychological tendencies that seem to control your life. The Midheaven placement reflects both its sanity and neurosis. This book will show you the astrological signatures of your best (and worst) personality traits.

This is the only book written about this all-important point in the astrological chart. What's more, it brings together the best of psychological and astrological theory. Written by a trained psychologist, *Power of the Midheaven* offers practical methods for identifying the most common mental processes for each Midheaven sign, both neurotic and healthy. Then it suggests the means for overcoming destructive habits that limit personal creativity.

About the Author

A professional astrologer for over twenty-five years, Stephanie Jean Clement, Ph.D., has been a board member of the American Federation of Astrologers since 1991. She has lectured and given workshops in the United States and Canada on psychological counseling and astrology. Stephanie's published books include *Charting Your Career, Dreams: Working Interactive*, and *What Astrology Can Do for You*. In addition, she has published numerous articles on astrological counseling, charts of events, and counseling techniques.

Stephanie's Ph.D. in transpersonal psychology has prepared her to work with clients in defining their creative potential and refining their creative process. This work is the source of her personal insights into vocation in terms of both practical consideration and spiritual mission. She developed a therapeutic technique for overcoming writing blocks and taught writing at the Naropa Institute in Boulder, Colorado, where she was an associate professor and librarian. She is on the faculty of Kelper College, an astrological college in Seattle, Washington.

To Write to the Author

If you wish to contact the author or would like more information about this book, please write to the author in care of Llewellyn Worldwide and we will forward your request. Both the author and publisher appreciate hearing from you and learning of your enjoyment of this book and how it has helped you. Llewellyn Worldwide cannot guarantee that every letter written to the author can be answered, but all will be forwarded. Please write to:

Stephanie Clement
℅ Llewellyn Worldwide
P.O. Box 64383, Dept. 1-56718-147-3
St. Paul, MN 55164-0383, U.S.A.

Please enclose a self-addressed stamped envelope for reply,
or $1.00 to cover costs. If outside U.S.A., enclose
international postal reply coupon.

Many of Llewellyn's authors have websites with additional information and resources. For more information, please visit our website at www.llewellyn.com

POWER
OF THE
MidHeaven
The Astrology of Self Realization

STEPHANIE JEAN CLEMENT, PH.D.

2001
Llewellyn Publications
St. Paul, Minnesota 55164-0383, U.S.A.

Power of the Midheaven: The Astrology of Self-Realization © 2001 by Stephanie Clement. All rights reserved. No part of this book may be used or reproduced in any manner whatsoever, including Internet usage, without written permission from Llewellyn Publications except in the case of brief quotations embodied in critical articles and reviews.

FIRST EDITION
First Printing, 2001

Cover design by Anne-Marie Garrison
Editing by Andrea Neff and Eila Savela
Interior design by Eila Savela

All horoscope charts used in this book were generated using WinStar Plus © Matrix Software

Library of Congress Cataloging-in-Publication Data

Clement, Stephanie Jean.
    Power of the midheaven : the astrology of self-realization / Stephanie Jean Clement.—
1st ed.
        p. cm
    Includes bibliographical references and index.
    ISBN 1–56718–147–3
        1. Midheaven (Astrology) 2. Self-realization—Miscellanea. I. Title

BF1718.5 .C545 2001
133.5—dc21   00-048142

Llewellyn Worldwide does not participate in, endorse, or have any authority or responsibility concerning private business transactions between our authors and the public.
    All mail addressed to the author is forwarded but the publisher cannot, unless specifically instructed by the author, give out an address or phone number.

Llewellyn Publications
A Division of Llewellyn Worldwide, Ltd.
P.O. Box 64383, Dept. 1-56718-147-3
St. Paul, MN 55164-0383, U.S.A.
www.llewellyn.com

Printed in the United States of America

Other Books by Stephanie Clement

Charting Your Career (Llewellyn Publications, 1999)

Dreams: Working Interactive (with Terry Lee Rosen) (Llewellyn Publications, 2000)

What Astrology Can Do for You (Llewellyn Publications, 2000)

This book is dedicated to my dear friends and teachers,
Wayne and Patricia Stauffer and Eleonora Kimmel.

Contents

Illustrations

Acknowledgments

The inspiration for this book came from the challenge of an astrologer many years ago who denied any significance for the Midheaven in delineation—an astrologer who had Neptune conjunct his MC. I took up the challenge, listening to everyone who had anything to say on the subject. In particular, I recall Mary Schneider giving a humorous talk that pointed out the soft spots each person has where the Midheaven is concerned. I also read Reinhold Ebertin's work *Combination of Stellar Influences*, with particular attention to the MC. In fact I have borrowed his language to provide headings for some of the sections of the book.

This book is designed for any astrologer to learn about the Midheaven. It also will help to define ego-consciousness and self-awareness in astrological terms. The professional astrologer is constantly called upon to counsel clients and even to provide therapeutic support. The Midheaven can be used to delineate what the client can learn about him or herself, distinct from what the astrologer learns from the Sun, the Moon, the Ascendant, and the planets. What you know about yourself determines what you can become.

Charts Used in *Power of the Midheaven*

Unless otherwise noted, all of the chart data in this book is from *AstroDatabank*. I owe a debt of gratitude to Lois Rodden for her lifelong effort to gather, verify, and compile birth data for astrologers. All charts in this book were calculated with WinStar Plus, a product of Matrix Software.

Introduction

WHAT IS THE MIDHEAVEN?

When I first began studying astrology, everyone learned to do the math. At that time there were no personal computers or computer services, and no one was willing to do the math for me. That meant that during the first ten-week class I ever took, I learned about birth time, Greenwich Mean Time, sidereal time, and interpolation using logarithms. I also learned that all this math served to compute the precise Midheaven in the birth chart, because the accuracy of every astrological chart depends on an accurate Midheaven.

Imagine my surprise when my teachers skipped over this point when they taught delineation! Oh, they didn't entirely discount its value. It was, after all, the most elevated point in the chart, as well as the cusp of the tenth house. However, I never was taught the in-depth delineation that we find in every book concerning the Sun, the planets, and the Ascendant. Entire books are dedicated to the Moon's nodes and Trans-Pluto, but none to the Midheaven. I was even told by more than one astrologer, when I asked about the importance of this point, "Oh, it's just important in the calculation. You don't need to worry about it after that," and, "Midheaven? What's important about the Midheaven? I don't consider the Midheaven." (This last remark came after a workshop in which over an hour had been spent delineating the Ascendant and its importance.)

As a beginning astrologer, I didn't really know what to make of the first remark, "Don't worry about it. It's only important in the calculation of the chart." After over twenty years in astrology, I know that no point in a chart is unimportant. Some points are more significant than others in an individual chart, but an accurate Midheaven provides as much valuable information as the Ascendant or any of the planets. In progressions and directions I don't know what I would do without this point.

As to the second remark, "What's a Midheaven? I don't consider it," this remark came from an internationally famous astrologer who should have known better. While this person had Neptune at the Midheaven, I don't feel that is any excuse. Telling students to ignore the angle which determines the orientation of the entire chart is not logical. It's like saying, "The wheels? Oh, don't pay any attention to them. They are just the part that connects the car to the ground. They are not important." When we are skilled enough to ignore the tires, we can fly. Without wheels we could have no car. Without the Midheaven we would have no chart.

Ignorance of the Midheaven and its meaning is a dangerous thing. We will be clever enough to ignore our own Midheavens only when we have achieved the level of integration that I discuss throughout this book. We will never actually be able to ignore the Midheaven in an astrological chart because we will not have that level of awareness of another person's psyche. The Midheaven provides data that is not available from any other source in the chart.

The Midheaven in Astronomy

The *meridian* is defined as the circle of longitude which passes from the South point of the horizon, through the zenith to the North point of the horizon. The Sun is on the meridian at apparent noon. Because the meridian follows a longitudinal line, we know that it is a great circle of Earth that intersects the North and South Poles. We see these longitudinal lines on globes and maps, usually for each fifteen-degree segment (or one hour) of the globe. The Greenwich Meridian and the International Date Line form one such great circle.

The *zenith* should not be confused with the Midheaven. The zenith is the point directly overhead for any point on the planet. It is the closest point on the meridian to the native. Whatever star or constellation occupies the zenith at the birth time is probably very significant, but it is seldom considered. Has any astrologer ever told you what star is closest to the zenith in your chart? You can find it by looking at a star map, using your sidereal time of birth. Locate the sidereal time in hours and minutes around the curved edge of the star map. Then move toward the pole until you come to your birth latitude. That part of the sky was exactly overhead when you were born. The zenith and the Midheaven are the same in only one case: when the ecliptic is directly overhead.

The *Midheaven* is the point where the meridian intersects the ecliptic. Put another way, the Midheaven is the point on the ecliptic that was due south at the time of birth. The Ascendant, by contrast, is the point on the eastern horizon at the birth time. If you have calculated many astrological charts, you know that the Midheaven and Ascendant are sometimes but not always ninety degrees apart. In chart 1 the ecliptic is aligned so that north-south and east-west lines divide it into four equal segments. In chart 2 (the same birth time at a different location) the segments are not equal. Thus we find that the relationship between Midheaven and Ascendant is not constant, nor simple. The complexity of this relationship is the foundation of individual differences.

Natural Meridian Cycles

Because the Sun follows the path of the ecliptic, we experience seasonal weather that affects the growing season and, indeed, all life cycles. The variation in the tropics results in smaller temperature differences than in northern or southern regions. In the temperate zones the position of the ecliptic defines spring, summer, autumn, and winter very clearly.

Every day at noon, local mean time, the Sun is in the Midheaven and defines the north-south axis geographically. In the Northern Hemisphere, if the Sun is in Capricorn at noon, then it is winter. If it is in Aries, then it is spring. In the Southern Hemisphere we find the opposite. If the Sun is in Cancer at noon, it is winter, while the Sun is in Libra at noon in spring. A person born at noon on June 22 will be in tune with the energy of the solstice in a different way from a person born with the Sun in any other position. A person born with the Sun conjunct the Midheaven will be in touch with his or her own personality in a very different way from the rest of us who have the Sun in any of the other 359 degrees of the zodiac.

Two kinds of motion affect the Midheaven—zodiacal and diurnal. On a given day at a given time the planets can be found in a specific degree of the zodiac.

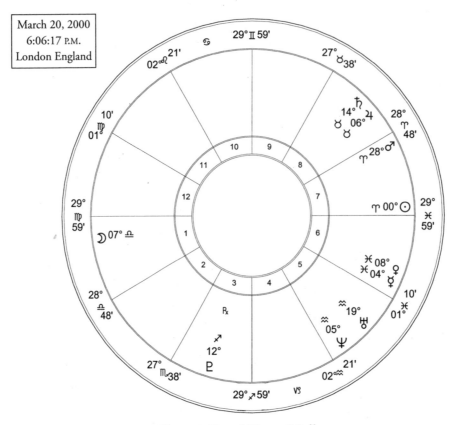

Chart 1. Equal House Midheaven

Throughout a day the Midheaven will move through all degrees of the zodiac. We calculate sidereal time in order to determine which degree is in the south at the birth time. The Midheaven moves forward through the zodiac at approximately 1 degree every four minutes. The result of this is that the planets, while moving slowly forward through the zodiac, move backward in relation to the angles in the chart. Thus a person born at 10:00 A.M. will have the Sun in a later zodiacal degree from the Midheaven, while a person born at 2:00 P.M. will have the Sun at an earlier degree. While the relationship between planets changes relatively slowly, the relationship of the planets to the angles changes quickly, hence the dramatic differences between individuals born on the same day.

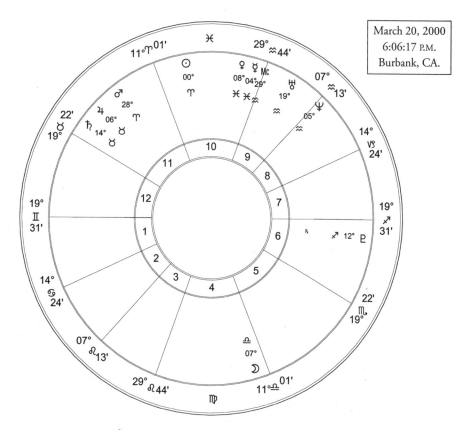

Chart 2. Unequal House Midheaven

The Midheaven in Astrology

We cannot consider the Midheaven separately from the rest of the chart, but must see it as part of the overall pattern. Yet, in developing a sense of what the Midheaven represents, we will examine it as distinct from other significant points in the chart. Please remember, however, that the Midheaven is part of a larger whole. The Midheaven represents ego-consciousness—what we know about ourselves. We know that the ego is not the entire being, yet the Midheaven is an essential part of the chart, the same as the Sun, Ascendant, or any other planet or angle.

The pattern of the horoscope reflects our individuality. When we are centered in that individuality, we can function at the highest level. In a geocentric chart, Earth is at the center, and the focus of that center is the place on Earth where the native was born. Thus, we are each at the center of our own charts, represented by the full astrological map. The angles and planets indicate how we are each oriented toward the universe.

It is the purpose of this book to reveal the importance of ego-consciousness through study of the Midheaven. Light is shed on the chart through the Midheaven. Each individual knows himself or herself through the Midheaven. The most powerful self-expression is directed through the Midheaven. The importance of the degree and sign of the Midheaven cannot be overestimated.

The Midheaven Is Not the Sun

I have used the Sun at noon to explain how the Midheaven is found and to relate the chart to the seasons. I also indicated the significance of the angle between the Sun and Midheaven in terms of time of day. The Sun is in the Midheaven only for people born very close to noon. The energies of the Sun and Midheaven are more closely aligned if the Sun is conjunct the Midheaven. For most people these two points are not only different, their angular relationship indicates the divergence between the vitality of life and what we know about that life. We know people who have little physical vitality, and yet live full lives, ignoring their limitations. We also know people who appear to be strong, vital people, yet live limited lives, believing they are not able to do or to be more. In the first case, people know that they can do whatever they want, regardless of the physical constraints of limited vitality. In the second case, people are not living up to their potential, but restrict self-expression because of a lack of self-knowledge.

Many years ago a teacher explained that the Sun indicates the potential you are born with, good and bad. As you grow, you discover that other people like some of your individual traits and dislike others. You then gravitate toward the Ascendant, selecting those traits of the rising sign which please the other people in your environment. Hence, you develop a personality which capitalizes on those qualities which you want to show to others. Later in life you move back toward the Sun, learning the highest physical, mental, emotional, and spiritual expression of the Sun sign.

The Midheaven and Ego

Now, let's extend this explanation to the Midheaven. We are born with very little capacity to distinguish Self from Other. We have been a part of the mother up to the moment of birth and continue to be very close to her, unable to survive without her nurturing. As we experience the world, we begin to be aware of our separate existence. We begin to act independently. We begin to become more self-aware. In short, we develop a personal ego-consciousness.

Throughout our lives we work with ego. It can be flexible or it can become rigid, due to personal experiences and our reactions to them. The more limited our self-awareness, the more painful existence becomes, and the less fully we express our individual potential. By the same token, the broader and more flexible our self-awareness and our willingness to become self-aware, the higher and more profound our ability to express personal potential in every area of life. The development of self-awareness depends on every angle and planet in the birth chart, but it is embedded in the Midheaven—the ability to mediate between the world of Self and the world of Other. In addition, self-awareness depends on the ability to recognize that what we are aware of is not the entirety of ourselves. We must be able to mediate between consciousness of Self and the profound inner depths of the unconscious psyche and the Collective Mind.

When Buddhists and other religious teachers ask us to achieve egolessness, they are really asking us to approach a state in which ego no longer rules our lives. As long as we are in physical bodies in an apparently material world, we need the ego complex in order to understand our position relative to other people and to the physical world. What we do not need is a rigid ego that admits no new ideas and feelings or does not process thoughts and emotions as fully as possible.

The goal is to end suffering rather than to end pain. Pain is part of physical reality, while suffering results from inadequate processing of a rigid ego complex. Suffering is an emotional reaction to pain, rather than a fully engaged response. I recall when my grandmother was dying. She was evidently in great physical pain, and I had difficulty watching her suffer. Yet she said, "Don't worry, Stephanie. It's not really that bad (the pain). And besides, I am ready to die." What appeared to be suffering to me was, in her experience, only pain. Then, when she died, I felt the pain of that loss, but I did not suffer very much because, I think, I had seen her death process and participated in it. I understood what was happening. For me, with my Aquarius Midheaven, understanding (knowing) alleviated suffering. It may be that each Midheaven has its own style of understanding that then relieves personal suffering.

Having said all that, I must say that I am still alive, I still have an ego and ego-consciousness. I also have less unnecessary suffering, at least at this particular time of my life.

Ego and Ego-Consciousness

The definition of the Midheaven begins with an understanding of ego and individuation. These subjects are explored from both Western and Eastern perspectives, thereby placing the Midheaven among the planets and Ascendant as a significant astrological indicator of personality and self-expression.

Webster's Dictionary defines "ego" in mostly Freudian terms: "[T]he self especially as contrasted with another self or the world," and "The one of the three divisions of the psyche in psychoanalysis theory that serves as the organized conscious mediator between the person and reality, especially by functioning both in the perception of and adaptation to reality." The "id" is defined as "one of the three divisions of the psyche in psychoanalytic theory that is completely unconscious and is the source of psychic energy derived from instinctual needs and drives." The "superego" is defined as being "only partly conscious, represents internalization of parental conscience and the rules of society, and functions to reward and punish through a system of moral attitudes, conscience, and a sense of guilt."

The first definition of ego—the self—is not accurate. The ego is only a part of the psyche, while the Self is a central part, thought by some to be the whole of the psyche, including all mental and emotional functions. Freud's self is a limited expression of being. Ultimately, the Self is not the whole either. The whole being is inclusive of physical, mental, emotional, and spiritual components. Freud's psychology never dealt adequately with at least two of these—the physical and the spiritual. When I think of myself I certainly include these.

The second definition, from psychoanalysis, is also inaccurate. While the ego (or ego complex) does serve as a mediator between the person and the outer world, that is not all that it does, nor is it the most significant function. Furthermore, reality cannot be defined as existing only in the outer world. My personal reality depends on my personal thoughts and feelings. Your personal reality is different. No one ever experiences a truly objective reality. The Freudian definition has one-third of our psyches mediating between something outside that none of us will ever perceive clearly, and the other two-thirds dealing with mostly or completely unconscious material. Freud stated that our needs and drives come from the id, a fully unconscious psychic element, while our morals, conscience, and sense of guilt come from a partly conscious internalization of someone else's beliefs. This Freudian apparatus would leave us powerless to function consciously—but we are not powerless. Therefore, Freud's definitions are inadequate to our present purpose, which is to consider the Midheaven as an indication of ego-consciousness, or what we know about ourselves.

Individuation

Carl Jung, a student and successor to Freud, offers more useful considerations. He begins with the concept that one of life's most profound goals is individuation, and that ego-consciousness is one of our most powerful tools in this endeavor. He defined individuation as "bringing to fulfillment the collective as well as the personal qualities of the person" (Bennet, p. 171). This brief definition of individuation overcomes the limitations of Freud's definition because it includes both a personal and a universal component. It also indicates that both of these are to be sought after and fulfilled. They are both worthwhile. Freud's definition of "self" suggests that our personal being is mostly unconscious and mostly bad, but here we find the beginnings of a sense of personal value. In addition, we sense that we belong in the larger scheme of things.

"Striving for fulfillment . . . is inherent in everyone. This may never be accomplished; but it is the aim of the process of individuation" (Bennet, p. 171). Unlike cookies, we are never "done." At different stages of development, how we strive will change. At some stages we appear almost as unconscious as Freud asserted. Small children strive to meet basic desires and needs. They develop an organized ego complex at about age six or seven. They relate to others intellectually in the teens, and develop social interactions into the twenties. Understanding of life's purpose emerges as late as the first Saturn return, and understanding of a larger purpose may only develop fully after that. While we carry unconscious material, both personal and collective, with us throughout life, we surpass Freud's definition of ego very early in the developmental process and begin working on the fulfillment of our potential on a deeper level.

"The process of integration of the world of consciousness and the inner world of the unconscious" is integral to Jungian psychology (Bennet, p. 172). Freud would agree that it is important to bring our unconscious material into consciousness so we can work with it, and he would agree that the ego complex serves the function of aiding in this process. A substantial difference lies in the fact that Freud conceives of reality as separate from the individual, while Jung states that the finest work takes place within us.

"In healthy people there is a shift in the center of gravity of the personality and the ego is superseded by a less ego-centered, that is a non-personal or not exclusively personal center—the Self" (Bennet, p. 173).

The Self also is the center around which the whole being is organized. Each factor in the astrological chart indicates physical, mental, emotional, and spiritual levels of being. The personality is composed of indicators which astrology identifies as follows:

Quality of Personality	Astrological Indicator
Persona, what we show to the world	Ascendant
Ego-consciousness and spiritual awareness	Midheaven
Being, spirit, mind, masculine aspect	Sun
Subconscious soul, feminine aspect	Moon
Awareness of other	Descendant
Collective foundation	Imum Coeli (the Midheaven)
Intellect, mediation	Mercury
Love, attraction	Venus
Physical energy, determination	Mars
Awareness of law, harmony	Jupiter
Perception of structure, inhibition	Saturn
Awareness of change, intuition, independence	Uranus
Receptivity, mystical awareness	Neptune
Force, power	Pluto
Capacity for association with others	North Node

These components are composed into a whole within the framework of the zodiac which reveals multiple expressions of each fundamental potential. The above list is not intended to be a complete list of qualities; it is focused on some of the primary factors considered in astrological charts.

Not much attention is given to the center of the chart in astrological writings, yet it is very significant indeed. The center of a geocentric chart is Earth and, more specifically, the point on Earth where the individual was born. Hence, the individual is at the center of the chart. Whole therapies have evolved around the concept of centering as a desired outcome, and it is no different in astrology. Jungian analytical psychology seeks to reveal a center that is the Self. Astrology helps us identify the "being," which includes the Self and all those other principles necessary to life.

"Individuation implies a living relation between the conscious and unconscious. The more we become conscious of ourselves, through self-knowledge, and act accordingly, the more the layer of the personal unconscious that is superimposed on the collective unconscious will be diminished. In this way there arises a consciousness which is no longer imprisoned in the petty, over sensitive personal world of the ego, but participates freely in the wider world of objective interests. The complications . . . are no longer egotistic wish-conflicts" (Bennet, p. 173). Here we find Jung at once acknowledging the limited consciousness of which Freud spoke, and at the same time indicating the direction we take to overcome limited mind. It is through active conversation between conscious and unconscious that we clarify our personal relationship to the universe. By diminishing, I do not think Jung means to reject or negate that material. Rather, it is our goal to reduce the obscurity caused by difficult personal unconscious material. To the extent that clarification occurs, the ego complex becomes more flexible, able to work with larger collective principles. Then personal issues occupy a smaller part of our world and we are opened to the full breadth of possibility. At this point, we begin to achieve our fuller creative potential which is revealed in the natal chart.

Buddhist Psychology

While Western psychology developed its definitions of mind within the last 150 years or so, Eastern philosophies have been working with these principles for centuries. Hindu and Buddhist concepts never separated intellect from soul. Rather, such a separation was seen as destructive. "As soon as we divide experience into perception and field of perception we are separating ourselves from experience. This is what is known as 'ego,' the condition of duality. . . . We have never been separated from our enlightenment but only seem to be so from the perspective of our obsessive attempts to divide experience" (Chogyam, p. 9).

While Western religion has devised a complex system of intercession to bridge the gap between us and God, Eastern religions have simply labeled any perceived gap as ignorance of the true condition. That ignorance is what they call "ego." Therefore, what we identify as the very way we understand the world they label as ignorance or obstruction of the truth. "Form is emptiness and the very emptiness is form; emptiness does not differ from form, form does not differ from emptiness; whatever is form, that is emptiness, whatever is emptiness, that is form, the same is true of feelings, perceptions, impulses and consciousness" (the *Heart Sutra*). Form and emptiness are one—feelings and emptiness, perceptions and emptiness, impulses and emptiness, consciousness and emptiness—are all one. This is no easy concept to grasp. We think about it for a few minutes and go back to figuring out how to get a larger or more meaningful share of feelings, perceptions, or whatever.

These two quotations, one contemporary and one dating from about A.D. 500 reveal a Buddhist teaching concerning ego. The most basic principle is that Unity exists and we are separated from it through our own perceptions. The condition of duality is what we depend on for our physical existence, yet duality itself does not exist. Our suffering comes from the feelings, perceptions, impulses, and consciousness of duality. Ego is the very condition of duality.

Western psychology suggests that we work with ego-consciousness in order to relieve inner conflict. Jung mentions the process of integration of conscious with unconscious. The Buddhist teaching suggests that everything is integrated already.

The ancients had no clear boundaries between themselves and the gods (or nature). They were in direct contact with the earth and its energies in ways that contemporary psychology might consider pathological. They "spoke" to the earth, they felt the energy of their medicine bundles, and their animistic world view gave life and personality to the energies around them. Their gods were the embodiment of the power of nature which they could not control, but which they sought to understand and to propitiate. Those same gods and goddesses have been immortalized in the constellations that make up our modern zodiac and the rest of the heavens.

Early people did not separate conscious and unconscious. For them the medicine bundle was alive with power and spoke to individuals directly. The gods and goddesses were personified, but they were not so distant. Gradually, we have become removed from this direct contact with a part of reality, to the point where we no longer call it reality at all.

People seek, through the individuation process, to understand the world more fully. We do this by working with our personal unconscious material first. Individuation brings us into closer contact with unconscious material and allows us to feel a part of the natural phenomena round us. Then we are able to access the collective material which is the rich heritage of human consciousness as it has developed through prehistory and history. We are also able to value the particular significance of that collective mind for our individual situations. The more we understand the world—the less dense the veil of our own personal unconscious becomes—the more we can relate well with others and the more satisfying our being in the world will be.

We experience enough conflict in the world outside ourselves. The more we resolve our personal inner conflicts and develop a flexible ego—a flexible way of approaching the world of the Other—the less we must rely on old, rigid, no-longer-successful strategies for dealing with life.

Summary

"Ego" can be defined as that part of the psyche that aids us in becoming conscious of the world. It creates a boundary and interface between inner psychic life and outer awareness of "other." Ego-consciousness involves the growing awareness of how the ego works—what processes are involved in awareness of self and other. Ego-consciousness also involves the process of integration of conscious awareness with unconscious materials in that it is the ego complex that permits such awareness to develop.

At least two clear purposes for ego-consciousness are evident. First, we can meet the challenges of life with greater flexibility and creativity if we are aware of our own psychic processes. Understanding how we think and how our feelings are influenced by both conscious and unconscious material is essential. Second, we can appreciate the true nature of the universe and of the larger mind of the universe only if we appreciate the nature of personal consciousness. We use the sophisticated structure of language and mind, developed over millennia, to re-discover a simpler, more direct connection to the world around us. The Midheaven shows each individual's unique approach to these challenge.

The following chapters will include in-depth examination of the Midheaven in each sign. A number of the charts I have used are based upon speculative data—that is, one or more astrologers have examined biographical information about the individual and have determined the birth time based on the evidence. I have chosen people who I feel exemplify certain traits of each of the signs on the Midheaven, and I have included a list for each sign for further study. Sources of additional birth data are included in the bibliography.

1

THE MIDHEAVEN IN TWINS' CHARTS

The astrological study of twins has generally focused on finding the similarities in their lives that are reflected in their charts. Another area of delineation involves the identification of factors in their charts that explain their physical and developmental differences. No matter how identical the lives of twins are, differences in personality emerge. Individual will is the key factor in such differences. In the realm of physical strength and vitality, we expect strong similarities because the charts are so similar. The small differences help the astrologer to understand the nuances of twins' charts, but also serve to understand the individual as well.

Astrologers looking at twins' charts casually ascribe differences in personality and appearance to planets changing houses, or sign changes on cusps. My research has shown that neither of these changes is common in twin charts. Thus, other factors must be involved in the delineation of individual differences.

Many events, such as the death of the parents, will happen at the same time for both twins, but many other events are likely to occur at different times, and in different circumstances. Timing events using transiting aspects to the angles and house cusps seems the most logical approach for events that are different. Because the planets are essentially the same, aspects to planets will more likely be involved in events that are the same. In the case of major events, aspects to the Midheaven and Ascendant reflect the striking differences in personal experience of the event for the twins.

Twin Research

Because of the difficulty of tracking the lives of twins, the research was limited to the neonatal period. Charts were gathered for all twin births in Denver General Hospital for a period of years, and a few appropriate cases from other geographical areas were also considered. To be considered, information had to be provided for survival of the first six weeks of life, and in the case where a twin did not survive, information about the cause of death was required. Exact birth times were required. The event under consideration is the survival/death of both twins.

The charts for the twins were calculated using the Koch house system. The following factors were considered:

Astrological Consideration	One Twin died	Both Survived
Planet(s) changing house	76% (ave. 1.5)	15%
Ascendant changing sign	8%	15%
Midheaven changing sign	0%	10%
Interceptions changing	28%	25%
Intermediate cusps changing sign	20%	25%
Stationary planet(s)[1]	92% (Ave. 1.16,)	15% (no more than 1)
Ascendant aspects changing (from applying to separating)	76%	56%
Midheaven aspects changing (from applying to separating)	56%	44%
Planets at 0, 1, 2, or 29 degrees	Ave. 2.6	Ave. 1.8

---

1. A stationary planet is defined as follows: Mercury 20' of arc applying or separating, Venus 15', Mars 5', Jupiter 3', Saturn 2', Uranus, Neptune and Pluto 1'. The stationary period is defined this way because the relative speed of the inner planets is greater, and thus the apparent slower movement continues over a wider orb of movement. These orbs result in a one- to two-week time period in each case.

The factors that proved to be insignificant included Midheaven or Ascendant changing sign, interceptions changing, intermediate cusps changing, and aspects to the Midheaven changing. The most significant changes included planets changing house[2] and the appearance of stationary planets. In about half the cases of the control and research groups, the aspect to the Midheaven changed, with slightly more Ascendant aspect changes in the research group than the control group.

This research proved the validity of astrology for me and prompted my strong interest in the Midheaven. Even though the time differences between twin births were very small in many cases, the aspects to the angles changed in over half of them. The slightly more frequent Ascendant aspects in the research group are readily explainable: the Ascendant relates directly to the physical body. The insignificant difference in Midheaven aspects in survival rate nevertheless inspired my research into personality differences.

To conclude: Using the Koch house system, planets changing house between birth times and the presence of one or more stationary planets accounted for more than 98 percent of the cases in which one twin died. The stationary planet was a clear indicator for the medical cause of death.

Application of the Research

I then began to research case histories of biological twins, time twins, and event twin events. In all three types of charts the very minor changes can be used to explain very different results in the lives involved. I will explain the importance of the Midheaven through examples.

A Case of Meningitis

Twin boys were born February 24, 1977, in Denver, Colorado, at 8:45 and 8:46 P.M. by C-section. At the age of five weeks the first-born child developed meningitis (chart 3).[3] Considering the tiny differences between the charts (fourteen minutes of arc difference on the Midheaven), the astrologer cannot use ordinary delineation methods to delineate why one child contracted the disease and the other did

---

2. Planets changing house proved to be a significant factor using the Koch house system. Using Placidus, the research and control group numbers were both exactly 50 percent and, therefore, not significant.

3. The charts for the twins case studies are based on data provided by the twins' parents.

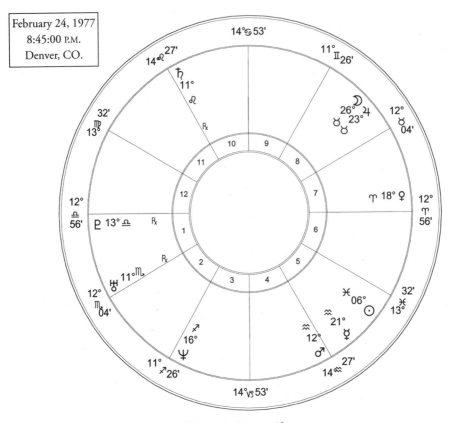

Chart 3. Twin Chart #1

not. On the day the illness began, transiting Pluto had retrograded to 12 Libra 54, exactly conjuncting the Ascendant (reflecting the physical body). In the second twin's chart this was a past transiting aspect on the date of onset (chart 4).

Where the Midheaven is concerned, I was very interested in what the mother had to say about the personalities of these boys. Astrologically, I considered the degree differences on the Midheaven. The first born has the Midheaven in the Sagittarius *dwadasamsa* (2.5-degree division of the sign), while the second has the Capricorn *dwad* there. I suggested to the mother that the second son would be more self-possessed (earth) and the leader of the pair (Capricorn ambition). The

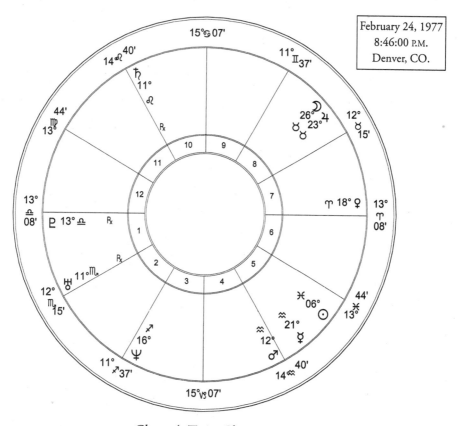

February 24, 1977
8:46:00 P.M.
Denver, CO.

Chart 4. Twin Chart #2

first would be more creative (Sagittarius would emphasize the loose fire grand trine). The mother confirmed that the second child was already the definite leader, and the contemplative, creative side of the first child was emerging.

From a counseling perspective, I was able to reassure the mother that the second child was not at risk for developing the disease, as the astrological indicators were already past aspects in his chart. I was able to indicate personality differences and offer advice about how to encourage each child as an individual, based on the change of degree on the Midheaven. The combination of reassurance and positive advice is the key to constructive delineation.

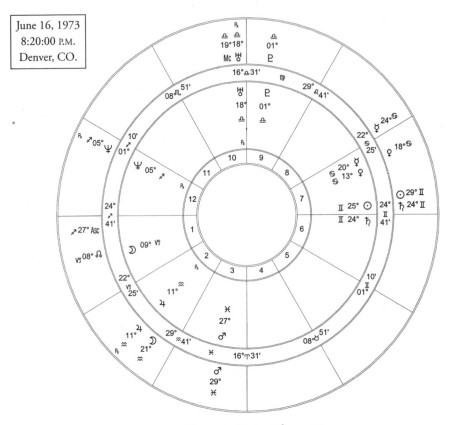

June 16, 1973
8:20:00 P.M.
Denver, CO.

Chart 5. Twin Chart #3

An Early Childhood Injury

Twin girls were born June 16, 1973, in Denver, Colorado, at 8:20 and 8:25 P.M. (charts 5 and 6). On December 26, 1976, the older twin fell and received a concussion and skull fracture. The mother was concerned that something similar might happen to the younger twin. Ordinary delineation of the planets in both charts by solar arc reveals the Sun at the critical 29-degree position, the Moon opposite Venus, Mercury quincunx the Ascendant, Venus square Uranus, Mars changing sign to Aries, and Pluto sextile Neptune. In the earlier chart the solar arc Midheaven forms an exact square to Mercury (nine-minute orb), suggesting overexcitement, and a semi-square to Neptune, suggesting recklessness. The progressed Ascendant forms an exact square to Mars (one minute of arc), suggesting a possibility of accidents and a sesqui-square to Venus, suggesting inner agitation and disharmony with the environment. All of this combined describes the accident clearly. The progressed Moon in the second house suggests that a personal belonging was involved: the child tripped on the hem of a nightgown while running

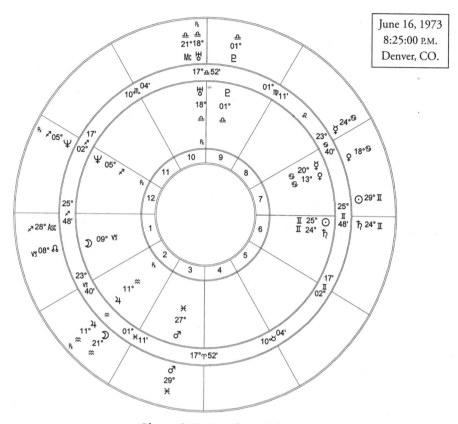

Chart 6. Twin Chart #4

through the house and hit her head (solar arc Mars has entered Aries). The progressed Midheaven squared Mercury, indicating careless or aimless behavior.

In counseling the mother, I first assured her that because of the way astrology works, the second child would never have the aspects that were indications in the accident, so it was very unlikely that she would have a similar injury. I then delineated the charts as I normally would.

The key personality differences included the following: the older daughter has the Midheaven in the Aries dwad, suggesting that she will be more energetic, more willing to experiment, and more aware of herself as an individual. The younger daughter will be more focused on establishing harmonious relationships, both with others and within her own personality. The less common sign change on the third–ninth house axis and the resulting difference in interceptions provides additional information which I will not expand on here. In this case these differences mark more pronounced differences in the chart than you can expect with most twins.

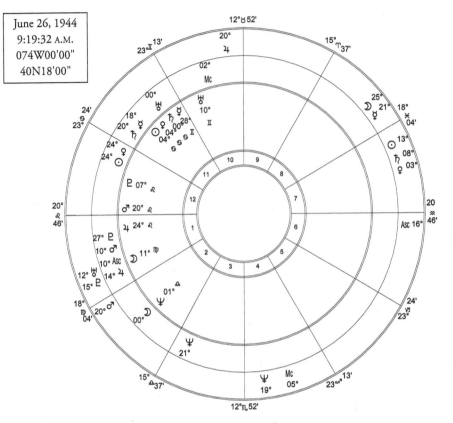

Chart 7. Twin Chart #5

Similar Events at Different Times

The birth of children is an effective tool in the rectification of birth times (charts 7 and 8). While twin births are carefully recorded, and generally the times are quite accurate, this example shows how rectification can work. Female twins were born June 26, 1944, at 9:20 and 9:30 A.M. Eastern War Time. Each gave birth to the first child on March 4, 1965, and March 27, 1962, respectively. Note that the younger twin had her first child three years before the older twin. This represents a reversal of the usual expectation that the older twin will experience events first. While there are numerous other aspects indicating these births, both sisters had the solar arc Ascendant square natal Uranus at the time their first children were born. This shows that the timing of events utilizes both zodiacal motion and diurnal motion. Adjusting the birth times in each chart, the solar arc Ascendant precisely squares the natal Uranus at 9:19 A.M. (with transiting Uranus trine the Midheaven) in the older twin's chart and 9:33 A.M. in the younger twin's chart (with solar arc Mercury sextile the MC).

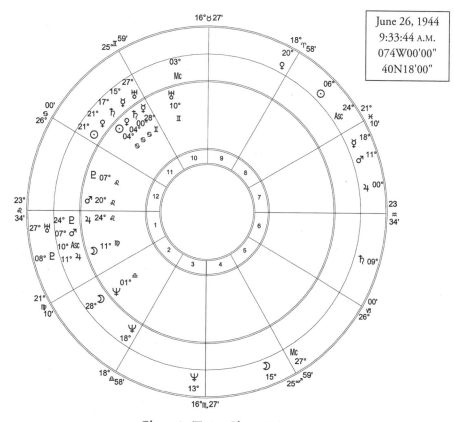

Chart 8. Twin Chart #6

Summary of Research on Twins

These examples of twins demonstrate the importance of the Midheaven in delineation. While events affecting the physical body include aspects to the Ascendant, the accompanying indicators of psychological involvement involve the Midheaven. The Midheaven offers rich information about individual self-awareness and how it changes throughout one's life.

2

EGO-CONSCIOUSNESS AND THE MIDHEAVEN

In order to make sense of the Midheaven and its place in the astrological chart, we first must understand what ego-consciousness is. In order to understand this, we must begin with an investigation of consciousness itself. While we think of consciousness in terms of thinking, learning, and reasoning, these things are not consciousness at all.

Consider learning first. Learning is an organic, nonrational process. Most of learning takes place outside of our conscious awareness. Examples abound. We learn to associate the taste of sweet fruit with initiation of the digestive process. Later the mere smell of the fruit can cause salivation. We did not learn this consciously, but on a physical level. Subliminal advertising or learning tapes attract a part of our minds which is not conscious. We learn to walk, dance, or engage in other physical activities on a bodily level, outside of what we think of as consciousness. Even when we are aware that behavioral conditioning is taking place, we cannot completely overcome the intended conditioning. Otherwise hypnosis would not work.

Consider another example: a diver is on the platform, waiting for her turn. We see her raise her arm, thrust it out to the side, pull it into her body. She kicks her leg up. She is consciously reminding her body of the more unconscious training that has led her to know how to execute the dive. Each movement connects the body with unconscious information that goes into the dive. The "conscious" part is her initiation of movement. The unconscious mind is responsible for everything else.

Thinking is another automatic process that requires little or no consciousness. We would be frightfully slow if we needed to consciously relate to each number in an arithmetic problem. We know thinking is unconscious when we jump to conclusions without following through an entire process. We are able to relate unconsciously to many and varied inputs in the solution of such a problem, arriving at an answer without focusing on every relevant piece of data.

Some say that reasoning is a conscious process. Actually what we refer to as reasoning is a very fast process that more closely resembles what we call intuition. There are two reasoning processes we all use. We are born with the capacity for inductive reasoning, and it is this method by which habits are formed. This is the method of reasoning that the unconscious mind employs. Inductive reasoning is a function of the weight of available evidence. The root word is the same for the term *induction*, which means "initial experience or initiation." The inductive reasoning process infers a general conclusion from particular premises. In the case of the formation of a habit, what worked in one case was presumed to work in other cases. As the weight of evidence of effectiveness accumulates, the unconscious mind generalizes the result to all similar situations, and potentially to all situations. As children we learn that ice is cold. We reason inductively that all things that look like ice are cold. We may find out that some ice-like things are warm, but we have reasoned before we touched the object that it is cold. Hence, we are sometimes astonished. Our reasoning has been based on experience. It is not as though we recall each time that we experience the coldness of ice, either. We simply make the judgment unconsciously.

The structure of our justice system is grounded in the principle of "the weight of the evidence." We are not asked as jurors to identify the truth. We are asked to make a judgment based on the evidence. Juries have been known to make decisions that seem to defy the evidence because they are making judgments unconsciously about the whole experience of a trial, not consciously focusing on discreet items of evidence.

Later in life we learn deductive reasoning, which involves logic. This is what we learn through language and education. The conscious mind is required to learn deductive reasoning. In deductive reasoning, the conclusion follows necessarily from general or universal premises. This kind of reasoning depends on the validity of the premises for the validity of the conclusion. In this kind of reasoning, all the available facts must be consistent with the conclusion. There is more conscious activity here, a formal process of consideration of a limited number of inputs. It is also true that if the inputs are faulty, the conclusions, while logical, will be incorrect. It appears that we can trust our (unconscious) judgment better than our (conscious) logic.

Reaction to stimuli is easier to accept as an unconscious process. When the doctor taps your knee, you react reflexively. You do not think about it. In fact, no amount of thought could completely stop the reaction.

We can use the Western management model to describe what we believe about consciousness. Major companies have a president or chief executive officer at the head of the company, while the body is made up of employees. Everyone looks to the president for leadership. A great deal has been written about the flaws in this management model. We have come to know that a lot of decision-making and most of the actual work takes place in the body of the organization.

Contrast this with the Japanese management model. At all levels employees are encouraged to provide input into product design, plant operations, sales, etc. In fact the whole company depends on this volume of input. Individuals are rewarded for ideas, and yet are expected to perform as part of a larger company. This is a more organic approach to operations. While it is hailed as a more conscious approach to management, it actually is using what we know about less conscious processes.

What is consciousness then? First, we are able to create spatial separations of mental contents through consciousness. These separations can be in terms of physical space or in terms of time. There are accepted values for normal separations. When our personal orientations establish conditions where the norm is unobtainable, consciousness can intervene and rearrange the internal landscape—reframe the data to suit our needs better. In addition, consciousness allows us to accept things that are otherwise unbearable. When Europeans went to Africa, they discovered that Masai people would die if kept in confinement. While Europeans had accepted confinement as a method of punishment, the Masai could not consciously accept such a limiting situation.

Consciousness also allows us to extract bits of information from a body of mental information. Memories of childhood events provide good examples.

When I was a child I went to the state fair, saw the animals, rode the rides, ate all sorts of food, but the clearest memory is of a pinwheel toy spinning in the breeze. I spun around and around to make it spin. The colors in my memory are so vivid that it is even better than reality. Going back to the fair as an adult is not the same experience at all!

Another example comes from law enforcement. Victims of violent crimes sometimes zero in on one detail of the situation, both to preserve their sanity and to fix that memory for all time. It could be a tattoo on the arm of the assailant, the shape of a car bumper, anything. They simply do not remember the whole crime and crime scene.

Consciousness further allows us to move these fragments around and to reorient ourselves with relation to them. If we have had traumatic experiences in the past, we can take the fragments we recall and place them into a different frame of reference. This allows us to heal old wounds and to arrive at forgiveness and self-understanding.

Changes like these require consciousness as a foundation. We make decisions consciously about past unconscious reactions. Choice resides, I feel, in consciousness. When we understand the connections we have created, based on our life experiences, we can choose to change those connections. This kind of understanding is on a conscious level; what we are trying to change may be unconscious.

Consciousness resides in the mind and in the body. Self-awareness allows us to integrate mind and body so that we no longer feel alienated from a part of ourselves. We need to feel like a whole being, not like powerless fragments of a whole being. We also need to be able to hear the voices from within us clearly, and to place what we hear within a flexible working framework which is our individual being.

Ego-Consciousness

With a more definite idea of what consciousness is, we can proceed to define ego-consciousness. With true ego consciousness we can discern the errors or non-functional connections that pervade our experience and limit our creative direction. Whatever misplaced fragments of information we find as we investigate our psychic landscape, we can consciously place those fragments where they belong. Barring that, we can restructure the connections around those fragments so that when we think of them we are led to wholesome, pleasant thoughts and feelings.

We can learn to understand the flow of time differently as well, placing events in an order that serves us more satisfactorily.

The creation of new frames of reference allows us to project creative energy into the future. For example, while we cannot work from the ground, of childhood abuse, we can work from the ground of occasional glimpses of our own power in childhood that helped us to survive. We can work from the framework of the creative unconscious mind that provided us with the wherewithal to survive to the present time.

Ego-consciousness allows us to investigate the interior landscape of our own minds. We can look at that which has been less conscious and we can see what it is and how it is. We can objectively examine inconsistencies. We can learn to appreciate those inconsistencies and gaps in the information we find. We can begin to love those gaps because they are now providing opportunities for change and growth. We can consciously determine how we want change to occur and when we want it, and how we will manifest it. All of this comes from ego-consciousness.

Relationship to the Infinite

As we are doing the inner work of defining and refining our conscious awareness, we are also opening to the infinite. Unconscious actions include reacting without conscious consideration of the consequences, overlooking meaningful connections between our own feelings and the exterior world, seeing the world in black and white only, depending on cause-and-effect relationships to explain the unexplainable events in our lives, and experiencing little or no creative choice. This kind of unconscious activity is limited and often pointless. We are unable to contact the infinite grace of the universe when we are in this condition.

As we become more conscious, our capabilities shift. We are able to respond more clearly. We begin to see connections between feelings and events and situations, and we evaluate them in terms of our conscious desires. We experience a fuller range of relational values, including a full color spectrum of possibilities and a sense of relatedness that no longer depends on cause and effect. Our appreciation for the richness of the world grows.

Finally, we are able to make creative choices, moment to moment. Instead of being caught in a swamp of unconscious reactions to disconnected events, we are able to choose to respond more wisely. We will still have angry, sad, unpleasant moments, but we will be able to choose to move past them into the creative field of awareness that we have cultivated.

The Encounter with the Infinite

If you do not understand yourself, you cannot know a relationship with the unlimited. If you do not understand yourself, you experience limitation—you react to the template of life (the astrological chart), but you are not engaged—the will cannot be properly engaged—in the experience of possibility. How does the psyche overcome apparent limitation and encounter the Infinite?

The center of anything is the meeting point of two vortexes. First, there is the vortex of all past actions which have brought you to this point: the focus and aggregation of all past thoughts, feelings, and actions which go into your personal experience. The natal chart is a focal point that represents your emerging consciousness at the moment of birth. Because it reflects all past events, it is an accurate map only for the birth moment. Second, we have the vortex of the future—the opening into wider and wider possibilities which all share the present moment as a starting point. From the moment of birth, things begin to shift—new moments of potential are continually emerging. This is why you must consider a person's historical progressions and transits, as well as the present conditions. Knowing what has gone before is part of a complete astrological analysis. No past events and conditions are uncreated. They had an impact when they occurred and continue to influence the individual in the present. The birth chart, when combined with progressions and transits, depicts the future possibilities for this nativity.

We cannot choose from among the possibilities of life when we are not self-aware. We can understand our personal past and future potential through ego-consciousness. We can see a map of future possibilities, and we can choose those conditions and opportunities that suit us. This is why every individual responds to progressions and transits in unique ways. We can generalize about prediction because of the nature of the planets and aspects; we cannot be overly specific about individual outcomes because we cannot predict the expression of free will.

What Do We Seek?

Most of us seek greater comfort, greater happiness, and more powerful opportunities to express our unique being. Each individual has a personal view of what constitutes happiness, success, or opportunity. Examination of a few philosophical/religious goals may help us develop a fuller idea of the possibilities.

Salvation

Christianity addresses the mechanics of salvation. If we try to do good and repent of our wrongdoing, we can go to heaven. We only need to trust in Jesus as our savior to be saved. There is also concern for others and their salvation. People can know us through our good works and thereby know God.

Liberation

Hinduism and Buddhism address the concept of liberation. People seek to escape the wheel of life to return to the source. In order to be liberated from the cycle of material existence, one will no longer be embodied as a part of creation. After that one no longer exists separately in any way. You cease to exist. This cessation is the goal of millions of people.

Enlightenment

Many religions and philosophies refer to enlightenment as the goal. Enlightenment involves knowing creation and identifying with it—becoming one with creation. There are two types of enlightenment. The first includes the self as part of the picture. You are able to see creation and know what it is. The second, a pure state of enlightenment, involves a loss of identification of the self altogether. In this case you will be saying, "I know that (creation), and I am that."

Realization

Realization is a fourth concept of major philosophies and religions. If the question is "What am I?" the realization is, "I am that which I create."

- I am the Source (being).

- I am that which is projected from the Source (thought).

- I am both that which creates and that which is created. Western psychology revolves around just this kind of paradox.

Understanding the Midheaven involves understanding the power inherent in this paradox. You and I are creators. We take what we have in the way of experience at any given moment and use that to create our futures. Not only do we do this, we always do the very best we can. We never shirk our responsibility to ourselves in this matter. We never intentionally identify what is best and then do something else. The principle of positive intent is immutable. If it seems that positive intention is not at the root of action, then we simply have not fully understood the action and its source.

You and I are also that which is created. We are the result of all our past thoughts, decisions, and actions. In addition, we are the result of the thoughts, decisions, and actions of our forebears to the extent that they were instrumental in creating us.

If we are both source and creation, there is no distinction. We have a problem with this principle because, in order to operate in the world, we polarize everything. We create distinctions where they do not exist. We separate ourselves from the past and the future in numerous ways in order to try to understand the illusion of that very separation.

A look at the zodiacal expression of ego-consciousness informs us about how the Midheaven relates to the rest of the astrological chart. We find that what we think affects how we respond to the planets and aspects. The key word here is *respond*. Until we understand the nature of the MC, we are reacting to the template, the planets, and their movement, with little or no consciousness. When we react, we come from a place of relative ignorance and often experience pain. When we respond, we come from a place of relative awareness and experience progress and success.

An example may be useful at this point. The first time I went to the dentist, I was scared silly. I didn't know what would happen, and no one had prepared me for the event. I had actually never seen a hypodermic needle before that day, nor had I seen anything like the equipment and chair in that room. I was, so to speak, relatively ignorant. No part of my education and experience had prepared me for that moment. I experienced intense fear, shame about that fear, shame that I had allowed a cavity to be created in the first place.

Now, when I go to the dentist, I take that experience with me, as well as many more. I know what the room will look like, I know what a needle is, I know about drilling and filling, etc. I am much better prepared by education and experience to deal with dental visits. In addition, I can tell my dentist about my past experiences. Now we can joke about the past and I can relax. I can say, "Remember that I don't really want to see the needle," and he often jokes, "What needle?"

I can relax because I know the procedure, and I can choose to engage in it, and respond to the situation instead of reacting to it.

The twelve signs, as they cross the MC, provide twelve patterns for the kind of understanding which human beings can experience. They provide twelve models for enlightenment, or twelve patterns for realization. Combined with the planets, signs, and aspects, these twelve models provide the myriad variations of self-expression and ego-consciousness. On the one hand, they indicate our limited understanding and the possible life experience we will have if we remain ignorant and reactive. On the other hand, they also indicate the path toward responsive engagement in the phenomenal and spiritual world as we become more able to respond to life experiences and to our role in the creation of those experiences.

The Nature of Resistance

Because resistance represents an obstacle to change within the psyche, it is important to have a very clear idea of what processes are involved. *Webster's Dictionary* defines "resistance" as "the inherent capacity of a living being to resist untoward circumstances (as in disease)." *Taber's Cyclopedic Medical Dictionary* defines resistance in this way: "In psychoanalysis, a condition in which the ego avoids bringing into consciousness conflicts and unpleasant events responsible for neurosis; reluctance of [the] subject to give up old patterns of thought and behavior."

I suggest a more useful definition: resistance is what we experience in the space between what we have had in the past and what we want now. It is the natural inertia of things: if space (in the environment, in time, or in the mind) is occupied by one thing, some effort is needed to move that thing aside to make room for a new thing (piece of furniture, activity, thought or feeling).

Resistance identifies a pivotal transition from what was to what can become. Resistance happens for us moment to moment. The MC provides a picture of how resistance works for each individual—a map of personal resistance "style." What is resistance? What is being resisted?

Resistance is the temporal transition between what exists and what we want to exist. Thus resistance is a part of the desire process. If we are ignorant of possibility, then we resist the future. We resist because we are afraid that nothing new can exist for us. We hold on to the past. The ways this holding on can happen are as numerous as people's thoughts. Each of us has a typical style of resistance which is colored by personal experience. This style can be modified through understanding, but it will remain a part of our personality at some level. Resistance can be reduced—we know, for example, that some kinds of wire conduct electricity, while other materials provide increased resistance. It is the same for the mind. Some situations are conducive to progress and some increase resistance to change. Understanding the MC helps us to understand our individual resistance style.

What is being resisted? We resist the displacement of ideas and feelings. Keep in mind that some resistance is a good thing: with no resistance thoughts would be completely random. The current moment is made up of stored thoughts. If we want to add something new to the picture, we need to create space into which the new "thing" can fit. The new thing seeks the center, and it must move something else out of the central position. It is the movement out of the center that is resisted, not the new thing. A little of this kind of resistance is good because it allows us to focus on one idea and hold it consciously.

Problems arise when we cannot consciously overcome the resistance. Suppose you want a new car. You begin to develop a picture of what this new car looks like. As the picture takes shape, you encounter resistance:

> That will be too expensive. (You do not want the money in your bank account to be moved out of the picture.)

> They don't make a color you like. (You don't want to give up the car you have because it was so nearly perfect for you when it was new, and you love that color. What you really love is the idea that that car was perfect and there can never be another one as perfect as that.)

> It will take too long to get. (You resist the time involved in making the agreement with the car dealer because last time that was such a painful process, and you don't know how to make sure you will like the process any better this time around.)

> You might wreck it and then where would you be. (You resist the possibility that you will mess up this new toy.)

The list could go on and on. The point is that resistance is about displacing more or less fixed thoughts that are tied to the past so that a space can open up for the future. Even the most open-minded person eventually comes to a point of limitation. We all share the common limitation experienced as physical death. No one yet has escaped death of the physical body. Individual flexibility determines how we deal with this and other lesser limitations in our lives.

Habitual Patterns

Why is it that people not only do not appreciate being told about their bad habits, but are hurt when we tell them the truth? Logically, we would think that if we have a bad habit, we would want to change it, get rid of it, or at least be aware of it. Yet, we are profoundly sensitive to the kind of criticism that strikes at our core habits. After all, while we cannot do much about height, and cannot take criticism about our height very seriously, we presumably can change our habits. That we do not is a very sensitive issue for most of us.

Why does it seem that people actually hold on to and protect these habits (or weaknesses) instead of willingly correcting them? Here we find the root of the issue. We have habits that no longer serve us well, but we hold on to them for dear life. We not only can't stop easily, we can't stop at all. We are addicted to our own bad habits—but why?

In the case of physical addiction, the body has established a need for the addictive substance. In order to cease consumption, we must go through a detoxification process in which we manage without the substance, cleanse it from the system, and, hopefully, develop new ways of being in the world that do not include the substance. We know, without doubt, that the addictive substance is not good for us—indeed, that it has harmful physical ramifications. Yet we know that quitting is no small task. The same is true of other addictive habits. We are "hooked." The habit, while not necessarily physically harmful, plays a role in our mental and emotional well-being. We can't do without it, any more than we can manage without the addictive substance—but why?

Except for addictions we are born with, all habits develop over time as responses to the environment. We meet a challenge, we try a coping tactic. If a tactic has worked in the past, we try it again in another situation. If it continues to work well, we use it in any situation that requires a response. At some point the conscious response becomes a pattern—it is more like an instinctive reaction than a planned response. As this shift from conscious response to unconscious reaction occurs, the habit is formed. It becomes an underlying strategy—an adaptation of behavior that now serves the function of preservation of the psyche, but that is no longer under conscious control. While originally the tactic was fully conscious, the habit, or at least the impulse to employ the habit, is not.

The key factor is that the habit began as a more or less conscious response to an immediate need. At that moment it was a beneficial action. It ceases to be beneficial when response becomes reaction, and when the reaction is used in inappropriate situations.

Suppose that as a child you did something naughty. When confronted, you wish to avoid punishment, so you simply tell a lie. If the lie works—that is, if you avoid the punishment—you may try a lie again when confronted with a similar situation. If the lies work again and again, you may develop the habit of lying, even when the truth would serve just as well, or even better. This habit is very disturbing to the people around you. They never know whether you are telling the truth or not. They find they cannot depend on what you say.

Over a lifetime you told lies that often saved you from punishment. You value the practice itself, and you know that telling the truth often leads to unpleasant confrontation. You may say to yourself, "Why bother with the truth? It is so inconvenient." In addition, the lying behavior is embedded in other behaviors. Any activity that has an element of role-playing presents an opportunity to exercise the habit. In your role as parent you lie to your children. In your role as executive you lie to your subordinates. In your role as friend you lie to your acquaintances. Eventually, in your role as a human being, you lie to yourself.

When confronted with this negative, even disgusting habit, you find you are unable to change your behavior. The lies roll off your tongue so easily that you simply cannot make yourself tell the truth, even when it doesn't matter. You may care that people don't trust you, but you are unable to change. When your boss points out the problem, you are still not able to drop this terrible habit. And you get so upset when people catch you in a lie—but why?

For your friend who has suggested that you stop the behavior of lying, deductive reasoning is being used. Your friend can see the logical outcome: All instances in which you lie to your friend are causing harm. Therefore, you should not lie. It seems so obvious.

For you, something different is in play. In your unconscious storehouse of information from the past, lying worked in an initial instance. It continued to work in similar instances. Inductive reasoning suggests lying is useful in all instances. For you the truth has little value relative to the potential for lying. Lying to your friend is not really a problem for you.

How to Change a Habit

When an unconscious dynamic is active, usually it is not possible to employ deductive reasoning to change the behavior. It is necessary to accumulate a weight of evidence that will swing the unconscious scale in a new direction. Because the information is unconscious, you may find that a therapist, counselor, or a large group of friends will have to help you, or you will have to act as your own counselor, amassing enough pertinent information to swing the unconscious scale yourself. This can be a formidable task.

How can astrology help? Astrology has two components that offer solutions: First, the astrological model can reveal the roots of the habit mechanism. It shows what habits are most easily formed, and reflects the metaphors for such habits. It suggests the kinds of situations in which the habit is likely to be used, and suggests closely related situations in which the individual may be able to substitute another habit, thereby gradually changing the balance of the evidence.

Second, the astrological model also supplies the dynamic means to change the undesirable behavior in the form of metaphor, story, and new situations that have the potential to be handled differently. The astrologer can supply many varied reasons for change, and can suggest the actual change mechanism. Multiple choices can be suggested, and the client can be encouraged to try them in a very conscious way. As this substitution process proceeds, the weight of the bad habit is reduced to a more suitable size. The habit may still work in some cases, but new habits are developed that work even better.

In the process of changing habits, you come to know more about yourself. You no longer unconsciously react to situations. You are more able to engage the conscious mind as you make decisions about how to respond to life's challenges. You develop habits that work better. These habits are just as firmly rooted in your unconscious as the old bad ones. The difference is that the new ones have developed out of a cooperative arrangement between your conscious and unconscious, and represent what you truly want for yourself. The old habits developed unconsciously at a time when you were less aware of your own true needs and desires, and as a response to pressing circumstances that were outside your control. The joy is that each time you are able to change an old, less constructive habit for a new, more creative one, you are establishing the truth, both consciously and unconsciously, that you are a capable human being.

The Role of Astrology

I believe we have evolved to the point where we can gain deeper self-awareness, and I feel that examination of the Midheaven will aid us in this quest. In the following chapters each sign will be examined as it pertains to the Midheaven. Clear distinctions will be drawn in order to distinguish the MC from the Sun, Ascendant, and other astrological contents. Observations will include:

- basic delineation of the MC by sign, and the fundamental expression of the MC;

- how resistance is likely to manifest for each MC;

- sanity and neurosis for each MC, and how to use astrology to overcome bad habits:

- spiritual awareness and how each MC develops it;

- how to cultivate the capacity to respond rather than react;

- how each MC gains awareness of personal creative potential;

- how the individual can directly affect the expression of free will.

Because this writer is an individual who sports a particular natal Midheaven, there is undoubtedly a slant to this work. Some effort has been made to overcome personal bias through conversations with other astrologers, psychologists, friends, and people in general. I will make no excuses for biases that exist. I hope that readers will feel free to inform me when they find my errors or limitations. This book reflects over twenty-five years of psychological and astrological study, as well as a lifetime of observation of individual styles of coping with life. Just like everyone else, I am a product of my life experience. No doubt the astute reader will find me revealed in my writing about ego-consciousness and the Midheaven.

3

ARIES
MIDHEAVEN

When Aries falls at the Midheaven in the Northern Hemisphere, the distance between the Midheaven and the Ascendant is generally greater than 90 degrees. At the equator the distance is between 86 degrees and 90 degrees. At 30 degrees north, the distance is about 90 to 96 degrees; at 40 degrees north it increases to about 100 to 108 degrees, and at 50 degrees north it is between 105 and 117 degrees. In the Southern Hemisphere the range is from about 57 degrees to 90 degrees, depending on the latitude. Thus the Aries Midheaven is always 90 degrees or less from the Ascendant there. With the Midheaven relatively close to the Ascendant, the person with an Aries Midheaven will always be somewhat more likely to initiate action then to respond to the actions of others. This self-directed tendency may be balanced if many planets fall in the western side of the chart because the planetary energies will favor the more responsive posture.

Placement of planets in the chart will affect this tendency. Planets in the Eastern Hemisphere tend to make an individual more self-directed, while planets in the Western Hemisphere indicate greater responsiveness to the environment. If the bulk of the planets support the wider Midheaven angle by falling in the Western Hemisphere of the chart, then the Aries Midheaven tends to be more extraverted. If most of the planets fall in the East, the individual will have a balanced ability to look inward for information and to respond to outside influences.

The Aries Midheaven exemplifies the capacity for self-establishment; awareness of one's own objectives, ambition, optimism, confidence; and a desire to lead others. Each of these terms is a name for a continuum of possibilities from the constructive to the less constructive. Less positive expressions include covetousness, fanaticism and rashness, to name a few.

Aries is a cardinal fire sign. On the Midheaven it indicates an individual who desires to fulfill the key phrase "I am." While the sun sign Aries may say, "I am," the person with the Aries Midheaven desires to demonstrate this capacity in every moment. Such an individual would say, "I know who I am." This person is very aware of his or her goals in life, and tends to approach them with confidence and optimism. For the Aries Midheaven, being told you are not—not old enough, smart enough, cute enough—can be devastating. The Aries Midheaven will proceed to prove that indeed the specified quality is there in abundance.

The desire to be what we perceive we can be is a positive trait. It provides the drive to learn and to practice skills. The pioneering spirit associated with the sign of Aries is implemented in a conscious, direct way to achieve one's goals. The limitation of this conscious drive is that it can become a compulsion. Pressing ahead with one's aims in spite of social or environmental signals to the contrary can result in accidents, for example. It is important not to lose sight of the ordinary care in our actions. Another difficulty is that self-awareness can give way to egotism, and when the ego is in charge, consciousness suffers. A resentful or argumentative attitude may arise when you don't get your way, and this does not endear you to associates.

Self-Establishment

The Aries Midheaven knows that becoming established in the world depends on personal effort. While the Sun sign Aries child may simply demand things ("I am hungry, tired, etc."), the Aries Midheaven will take the reins and actively pursue what he or she wants. Aspects to the Midheaven indicate the strongest, easiest, most direct methods for developing one's position, and progressions and transits indicate the most prominent timing of major changes in position. However, the Aries Midheaven has the force of the Mars ruler to energetically change conditions. Uranus. These two planets indicate the powerful potential of the Aries Midheaven to take an active role in mediating conflict and in establishing ritual as a social force through personal presence—through self-establishment.

Awareness of Objectives

Just as the ram must have a steady eye and a sense of direction, the Aries Midheaven knows how to set goals and pursue them. Ego-consciousness in this case includes a sense not only of the desired outcome, but also of the more likely ways to achieve objectives. In addition, the Aries Midheaven knows that the goal is self-generated. Many people allow their goals to be set for them, but not the Aries Midheaven. This individual will examine the possibilities and then may go off in a totally unexpected direction.

On the opposite end of the continuum, when the Aries Midheaven loses sight of goals, because of emotional upsets, changes in family matters or job, etc., he or she may feel ungrounded and very uncomfortable. There is a level of comfort about always having goals to pursue; when suddenly those goals are fulfilled or changes in one's life make them inappropriate, then the individual needs time to develop new directions. This process does not take very long; the Aries Midheaven will be irritable while it occurs.

Ambition

Once Aries Midheavens set goals, they pursue them zealously. These individuals are ambitious because they always have something they are going after. They may change their minds about what they want; they seldom are without some aim in life. When their aims revolve around the acquisition of things, they can err on the side of covetousness. As the desire for things occupies more and more of their thoughts, they lose sight of the higher spiritual goals indicated by the Mercury and Uranus esoteric rulers of Aries. They are fully engaged in the Martian use of energy to acquire. Here, as with all things, the Aries Midheaven will gain awareness of personal balance.

Optimism

In general, Aries Midheavens are optimistic, probably because they know they are in control of their lives. They have confidence that has developed throughout their lives that they can set goals and reach them; hence, they are happy to work on whatever activity will lead to success. The downside of such optimism is the fanatical pursuit of aims. Aries Midheavens can become consumed with an idea, leading them to ignore other people's needs, and even their own needs. Sometimes, regardless of how good they think an idea is, Aries Midheavens need to let go of projects that are interfering with the progress of relationships, health, and other significant areas of life. The Aries Midheaven can even let go of things optimistically because self-awareness has been developed.

Desire to Lead

Aries Midheavens know they are strong leaders. The capacity to take an idea and implement it often requires the help of others—Aries can certainly inspire people to action. There is also the knowledge that organizational skills have been developed which contribute to good leadership. When the goals are self-centered, Aries Midheavens can lead others into trouble; it is essential to set goals which are in the interests not only of the self, but of the group, the organization, and society in general. They must also learn that what works for oneself may not work for others; good leadership involves getting the best work from each person, even when that is different from the way one would do it oneself. The desire to lead must be backed up with organizational and communication skills.

Rashness

The Aries Midheaven can fall into the habit of charging ahead without adequate planning. Personal drive can be mistaken for practical considerations and good intentions. This is one area where attention to the esoteric rulers of Aries can help. These individuals can think about their role in mediation of whatever difficulties may arise in the execution of their plans; they can also employ ritual to create alignment between themselves and their employees. While these two considerations might not be personally necessary, they are essential to working with others. They also prevent rash decisions from causing difficulties.

Resistance

For Aries Midheavens, resistance involves dropping an idea, or allowing someone else to complete it, in order to go on to the next project. Aries Midheavens are most successful in the idea and planning stage of a project; if they maintain ownership of the idea, other people never get the opportunity to fulfill their roles of development and completion.

Because resistance occurs between what one has now and what one wants for the future, Aries Midheavens are not immune to the problem. They may be surprised that they get caught up in particular projects and cannot let go. They may think they have turned something loose and then find that they are still as emotionally attached as ever. Aries Midheavens know that they are good planners but they may not have any particular skill at letting go. Resistance will dissolve when the next idea begins to take form, and not until then. Don't expect an Aries Midheaven to hang out waiting for the next idea, the next project, without some friction.

Capacity to Respond

Fire signs in general, and Aries in particular, know that they can respond to problems effectively. They are very capable of developing plans to resolve difficulties in creative ways. When they are in a reactive mode, Aries Midheavens will fall back on patterns which were creative in the past but which do not suit the current situation.

Sanity and Neurosis

The three thinking styles associated with Aries at the Midheaven include the following astrological correspondences:

1. The cusp of Pisces and Aries, or the movement from mutable water to cardinal fire.

2. The pure energy of the cardinal fire sign itself.

3. The cusp of Aries and Taurus, or the movement from cardinal fire to fixed earth.

These three relationships describe both the neurotic potential of Aries on the Midheaven and the sanity to be found there.

Pisces/Aries Cusp

The movement from a water sign to a fire sign is the dynamic of discriminating awareness in Buddhist psychology. The movement from mutable water to cardinal fire is the transition from an emotionally impressionable state of mind to assertive expression of one's being. The foundation for this transition lies in receptivity to impressions, and requires a redirection of energy outward into the world. Ideally, this movement, on a deeper level, is from compassion for other people to effective personal action. It is clear that frustration can arise if compassion is strongly felt, but no effective means are available to act on that compassion. Such an individual may seek a career that has a body of theoretical and practical training in the requisite skills. Compassion can arise naturally in the form of intuition about the customer or client, and the appropriate skill can be employed to assist that individual.

The neurotic expression of this first Aries Midheaven thinking style lies in focusing on the desire itself. Compassion is out the window because the mind is filled with the desire to take action. Without the grounding of compassion, action has no meaningful goal. Oddly enough, the more the desire is emphasized, the less compassion remains. The focus is so much on the self and so little on the other that one cannot make progress, and frustration develops, leading to anger. The original compassionate response has only led to anger, but no effective movement toward fulfilling one's own desire or helping someone else.

As you will see with all the signs, the shift of awareness needed to resolve the neurotic pattern is not dramatic. The fulfillment of desire for the Aries Midheaven lies in incorporating both compassion and desire into one statement, for desire and compassion arise as one entity. The statement might be, "I know I am able to help this individual by mobilizing my own desire to act effectively." First identify with compassion. There has to be a willingness to focus on those feelings consciousnessly, and not merely in an intuitive sense. The resource for this objective view can be found in Libra, the sign on the Nadir. It may be helpful to objectify the feeling in some way. Even the mere naming of the feeling is helpful. Libra's ability to balance provides the framework for connecting feelings of compassion and desire in a meaningful way. There is an ability to see the larger picture in any situation. Then Aries' capacity to mobilize desire into action has something valuable behind it. Because the focus is on motion and change, the grounding provided by training is necessary. With no solid footing, effective action is difficult. Hence, the Aries Midheaven demands training of the mind and body to provide skillful means.

The well-rounded Aries Midheaven can become skilled in many kinds of careers. The best careers are in forward-looking services in which the individual works with others directly to accomplish just about any kind of goal. This could be anything from working on a production line in a factory, to selling perfume, to social work. The important factor is the direct relationship between understanding the needs of the end consumer and designing one's actions to work toward that need. There is greater personal satisfaction when the Aries Midheaven understands his or her personal contribution toward the end result clearly.

The unconscious skill that is associated with this personal work is the capacity for balancing more than one feeling and objectifying those feelings in some way. When the feelings just run around in one's head, they cannot be useful tools. Clear Aries energy assesses the facts of a situation and assigns no blame.

The feelings are seen as part of an overall snapshot of reality at the moment, and they then become a focus for the desire to move that reality in a positive direction.

The Pure Energy of Aries at the Midheaven

The second thinking style of the Aries Midheaven deals with the energy of the pure cardinal fire sign. Resting in the energy of Aries reflects the pure energy of the fire element as it expresses through the cardinal, or directed, quality. The wisdom of pure Aries is larger than the self-assertive capacity. The action so evident in Aries behavior is born from an initiative on the mental plane. In a relatively contained space the heat of mental activity can be the beginning of a reaction that only later becomes apparent in the material world. For the pure Aries Midheaven to manifest most effectively, initial containment of the idea helps it to "hatch," so to speak.

The power of pure Aries lies in discriminating awareness, and the Aries Midheaven knows this. There is a capacity to become intimate with people and ideas in order to understand the dynamics fully, and seeing the quality of things or people and the relationships between them. Flexibility and intimacy contribute to the compassionate warmth and empathy of fire signs in general, and Aries in particular. The development of discriminating taste provides the foundation for creative action that is fully effective, not destructive.

The destructive capacity is the peril of Aries. This Midheaven knows it is capable of causing harm in its overly enthusiastic effort to help others. The Libra Nadir provides the resolution of rashness in its refined, integrated mental activity. There is an honesty about Libra that emerges for the Aries Midheaven in clear intuition that can be verified through communication that implies no blame, but simply seeks to understand. Libra provides the moment of equilibrium in which decisions can be made. The contemplative interlude provides a pause between the inspired idea and its execution, thereby eliminating recklessness without dampening enthusiasm. The Libra understanding of duality allows the Aries Midheaven to integrate the mental processes before embarking on specific action.

The Aries Midheaven can benefit from learning a decision-making process that engages the mind. By taking the time to think through one's choices, decisions are based on a balanced assessment rather than on a single emotion. One choice is really no choice at all. Two choices create a dilemma. Three clear choices provide comparative ground on which dilemmas can be resolved. The

Aries Midheaven needs the patience to figure out the three choices, and the impulse to choose one of them.

Aries/Taurus Cusp

The third thinking style of the Aries Midheaven is concerned with the transition from Aries to Taurus, or from cardinal fire to fixed earth. In alchemy the relationship of fire and earth is one of hardening, as in the making of pottery. The smith puts the iron in the fire to temper it, and the Aries Midheaven puts its ideas into the fire to temper them—to remove emotions from the mix enough to see the concrete result of its actions.

There is also the action of reducing something to ashes. Clearly too much fire—too much anger or impulsiveness—can destroy the product or process. Too much energy may result in a superficial assessment of a situation—incoherent thought prevents effective action.

In the process of burning, boundaries become less distinct. The Aries Midheaven may need to cultivate a sense of beauty, an awareness of tastefulness. Then the tendency to arrogance is balanced by a desire to achieve elegance. The elegant Aries Midheaven always functions within the boundaries of tasteful behavior because of its ability to discriminate those actions and speech of others that reveal essential social mannerisms.

The neurotic expression of this Aries Midheaven style is arrogance. This unattractive trait may emerge when Aries is isolating itself from others, saying, "I am better than those people and must isolate myself from them." The sense of separation is an important part of the discriminating function, but can become arrogant when it is used in a judgmental fashion. A direct way to breaking this isolation is touch. Touch causes you to relate to the physical aspects of the world directly. It also aids in the integration of feeling and intellectual experience with the physical being.

Summary

In the positive expression of the Aries Midheaven, the act of being in the material world becomes the catalyst for intuition, intellect, and feeling to merge in the conscious expression of compassion in action. The Aries Midheaven learns to value the moment of clarity that arises in contemplation. Meditation that focuses on the breath can be particularly useful, because it addresses both the physical reality of life and the movement of change.

Conscious Choice

When an inspiration first enters consciousness, the Aries Midheaven experiences the fullest force of its creative power. This is the nature of intuition—to emerge as an idea or impulse so strongly that it captures conscious attention. The Aries Midheaven also knows how to flesh out the creative impulse with facts and figures, gathering the information and materials necessary to the accomplishment of the creative goal. The Aries Midheaven may also know that the power of creativity lies in an offensive posture, not a defensive one. They take an idea and run with it, not waiting to see if others will agree with their assessment. They may unconsciously sense the balancing factors that contribute to successful completion.

Spiritual Awareness

The Aries Midheaven has a spiritual awareness that grows throughout the lifetime. The intuitive sense of right action guides the conscious decision-making process, and thus the Aries Midheaven knows the proper direction naturally. The mechanism for spiritual awareness is the exercise of will. In the self-aware Aries Midheaven, courage guides action. In the unaware Aries Midheaven, the mechanism is dictatorial, revealing fanatical attachment to an idea for the sake of the idea itself, or because the individual cannot let go of personal ownership of the idea.

The Aries Midheaven realizes the fullness of spiritual possibility in much the same way they approach any creative process. They mobilize the will by identifying with the spiritual reality directly. Aries says, "I am that," and then becomes it. As this knowing of the spiritual path and goal develops, the Aries Midheaven is able to set aside petty frustrations of day-to-day activities more easily. They may continue to feel the frustration, but they do not entertain it. They simply acknowledge it as one step in the process. Selfish responses are replaced more and more with compassionate action.

Drawing upon the deep roots of the Libra Nadir, the Aries Midheaven understands the balance within all creation. They also relate directly to the moment of the spring equinox. The movement of the sun into Aries marks the impulse to creation and growth, and the Aries Midheaven understands this both consciously and intuitively. It is from this understanding that true compassion for self and others emerges.

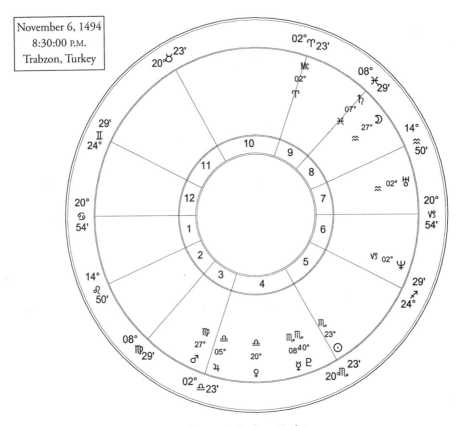

Chart 9. Sultan Suleiman

Suleiman the Magnificent

Suleiman was the ruler of the Ottoman Empire at its height (chart 9).[1] His father left him in the enviable position of having plenty of money, and he used it to consolidate his empire by codifying the laws and pursuing expansion of the empire. A strong warrior, he was able to conquer Mesopotamia (Iraq), Albania, and, for a time, Hungary. Some historians contend that Suleiman's father killed all of Suleiman's brothers and grandsons to insure his succession to power.

Data from Marc Penfield shows an Aries Midheaven, with oppositions to Mars and Jupiter, sextile to Uranus, and square to Neptune. Suleiman demonstrated his skill as a leader of the armies, and he managed the political intrigue of his court with some success as well. He knew he was meant to lead, both because

1. Information about Suleiman the Magnificent was gathered from the CD-ROM version of *Grolier's Encyclopedia*.

of his father's actions to assure his succession, and because of his own internal sense of self. He was able to harness the drive of Aries and not get caught in decisions that caused great losses in battle. He withdrew from Hungary and returned again later, better prepared.

The oppositions to Mars and Jupiter suggest that this well-educated man was able to also draw upon his inner resources of wisdom and energy. By codifying the laws of the empire, he consolidated his power. Others may have felt that creating laws would weaken their position, but he found that was not the case. He knew that to govern such a large empire, he had to have a system in place so that his Christian slave bureaucrats could manage things consistently in his absence. Not much is written about his actual spiritual practices, but he was a Muslim who spread the world of Allah and Mohammed to Europe and the Mediterranean. He was magnificent, but was the last of the great Ottoman leaders. After he retired from office, a bitter battle for succession ensued, with his weakest heir the victor.

Joan of Arc

As is the case with Suleiman, Joan of Arc's birth time is not certain (chart 10).[2] Lois Rodden quotes both 5:00 P.M. and 4:30 P.M. as possible birth times. Biographical sources suggest a birth time of one hour after sunset and numerous other possible times. The AstroDatabank time of 5:00 P.M. results in Jupiter opposing the Aries Midheaven, with Mars quincunx and Uranus sextile, indicative of the highly unusual and rebellious behavior of the Maid of Orleans. It is my opinion that Saint Joan exemplified the pure energy of Aries at the Midheaven, and therefore I favor a birth time closer to 5:30 P.M., but certainly after 5:00 P.M. by at least two minutes, placing the Midheaven in the second decanate of Aries.

Joan of Arc was the daughter of a peasant farmer. She began having visions and hearing voices around age thirteen. She kept this secret for five years, but finally was so certain of her knowledge that she was able to convince the French king to allow her to lead the army. Her military genius is reflected in the Aries Midheaven. Venus squares the Midheaven in the 5:30 P.M. chart, indicating the force of her conviction that she knew the will of God. If a birth time of 4:30 P.M. is used, then Neptune squares the Midheaven from the Ascendant side and Mercury squares from the Descendant side, reflecting her intense devotion to God and to France.

---

2. Information about Joan of Arc was gathered from the CD-ROM version of *Grolier's Encyclopedia* and *AstroDatabank*.

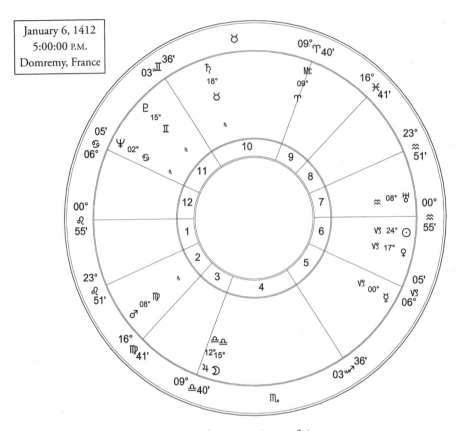

Chart 10. Joan of Arc

The danger of Joan's Aries Midheaven is that she will take rash action in the name of her beliefs, and that she will be too energetic in her desire to help others. The greatness of this Midheaven placement lies in her profound sense of honesty and forthrightness. Joan waited years before she left home to seek an audience with the Dauphin. Initially, she thought through her decision very carefully. Later she was consumed by her mission. After winning a victory at Orleans and seeing Charles crowned, Joan was captured in battle, thrown into a dungeon, tried as a heretic, and burned at the stake at the age of ninteen. Later, King Charles held a trial during which Joan was "rehabilitated," and she was canonized in 1920.

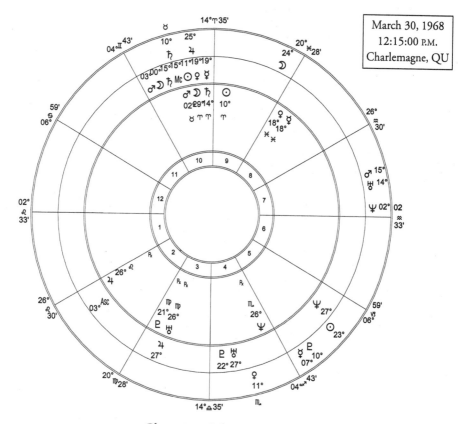

Chart 11. Celine Dion

Celine Dion

Celine Dion has captured the hearts of music fans everywhere with her impressive voice and deep understanding of the content of her work (chart 11).[3] She impressed the world with her decision to devote time to her husband and family as well. Whereas some careers can afford a two-year hiatus, performers generally want to stay in the limelight once they get there. It is much more difficult to re-enter the music profession once you have taken time out.

Yet, Celine decided that her husband and family are more important to her: "I've been given wonderful songs by the best songwriters in the world, and I've had the opportunity to perform these songs on virtually every continent. For now, I want to step back a little bit from the spotlight." She renewed her wedding vows

---

3. Information about Celine Dion, as well as the quotation, was gathered from the official Sony Celine Dion web site during February of 2000. The website is as follows: www.celineonline.com/bio_4.html

in a fabulous Las Vegas wedding that could have been taken out of the pages of *A Thousand and One Arabian Nights*.

Celine's Midheaven is at 14 Aries 35, with Saturn and Sun forming very close conjunctions. This Midheaven position reflects her capacity for discriminating awareness. In the midst of a skyrocketing career she was aware of her deep love for her husband and her mutual love affair with her fans. Able to see the relationships among various facets of her life, she did not let enthusiasm for one area define her life so closely that it destroyed another. The Libra IC indicates the deep well of love and harmony that guide both her career and her relationships. She no doubt agonized over a decision that ultimately was based on the balance of emotional factors. The decision was carried out through the Midheaven-Sun-Saturn conjunction, with her taking full responsibility for her decision. During the months leading up to Celine's retirement announcement, transiting Uranus, ruler of her seventh house formed a sextile to her Midheaven, and solar arc Venus, ruler of the IC, conjuncted the North Node of associations. Earlier the solar are Moon formed a semi-square to the Midheaven, indicating the stress she no doubt felt due to her husband's illness and her own impending decision.

Other Aries Midheavens

Salvador Dali, May 11, 1904, 8:45 A.M., Cadaques, Spain
Lauren Bacall, September 16, 1924, 2:00 A.M., New York, New York
Franz Kafka, July 3, 1883, 7:00 A.M., Prague, Czechoslovakia
George Wallace, August 25, 1919, 3:30 A.M., Clio, Alabama
Pablo Picasso, October 25, 1881, 11:15 P.M., Malaga, Spain
Alice Bailey, June 16, 1880, 7:32 A.M., Manchester, England
Prince Charles of England, November 14, 1948, 9:14 P.M., London, England
Lucille Ball, August 6, 1911, 4:00 A.M., Jamestown, New York
John Dee, July 13, 1527, 5:00 A.M., London, England

4

TAURUS MIDHEAVEN

When Taurus is at the Midheaven in the Northern Hemisphere, the angle to the Ascendant ranges from about 84 degrees on the Equator to about 121 degrees at 60 degrees of latitude. Thus, while Taurus is interested in personal comfort, there is a tendency to respond to others and to relate oneself to one's environment. Planets in the Western Hemisphere will reinforce this tendency, while planets in the east will support the more self-assertive style. Somewhat the reverse is true for southern Hemisphere births, where the angle between Midheaven and Ascendant ranges from about 85 degrees to about 43 degrees.

Taurus is a fixed earth sign. While the Sun sign Taurus may say, "I have," the person with a Taurus Midheaven will say, "I know what I have." Taurus the Bull, when in the Midheaven, knows his or her strength. The range is from powerhouse to puniness, but the Taurus knows this side of the physical and psychological make-up. The Taurus Sun reveals physical strength by its placement in the chart and aspects to it; the Taurus Midheaven, through its aspects, reveals what the individual knows about that strength. We occasionally see an individual who challenges all comers in spite of apparent physical or other weakness. We also see

39

people who are physically strong yet psychically weak; these individuals know only one side of their potential strength and refuse to acknowledge the other.

We also find people who are on the wrong side of their families and the law in their earlier lives, and who later "convert" their energies to the knowledge that they are part of a divine creation. We further find individuals who have staying power that is remarkable. Sometimes we are shocked when people "fold" on what appear to be very strong hands. The Midheaven in Taurus provides a map of the possible strength; the individual provides the choices for how to demonstrate that vigor on the physical, mental, emotional, and spiritual levels. The individual decides how long to hang on when the going is tough.

The Taurus Midheaven indicates an ideal positioning to understand the world of form. Such an individual has strong opinions about the physiology of life at every level. Here, again, the range of possibility is broad. Thoughts may center on the lowest level of form, doubting the value of creation and resisting anything that might seem frivolous in their own creative process. A higher expression may involve focusing on creative process in a deliberate, persistent fashion. Both types are seeking to produce in a meaningful way—that is, meaningful to the individual. The Taurus Midheaven is aware of inner creative potential; it is the use of individual will that guides this knowledge.

Preservation

The Taurus Midheaven knows something about preservation of objects, thoughts, and feelings. This individual knows that thoughts have life just as objects have existence. The stubborn quality of Taurus may lead to a belief that one's own ideas are the only good ones and that everyone else is wrong. In fact, Taurus may have lots of constructive and creative potential, yet some of their ideas are self-oriented and have no particular value for others. The Taurus Midheaven is invested in preservation of that which has been created, even when what has been created is a dynamic structure for change.

Persistence

The Taurus Midheaven knows that persistence is effective in getting results. The level of discrimination reveals the qualitative value of this knowledge. A more realized Taurus Midheaven may persist in a direction because he or she knows it has value despite apparent difficulties. The less realized individual may persist only because the path is known, and for no other reason. In this case, the individual digs into a situation that once served a good purpose, but which now could be replaced by more beneficial structures. Such a person can be intensely stubborn and needs time to meditate or otherwise create space for a new idea.

In fact, the Taurus Midheaven will benefit from the cultivation of mental space more than any other sign. Taurus, when he or she has considered a situation well, knows that a steadfast position is not only good, it is required. Someone has to provide consistency to the world. Never mind that others may see this behavior as stubbornness and inflexibility. The problem for the Taurus Midheaven is how to know when you have reached that truly "right" position.

Security

Taurus is always interested in security on some level, and the Taurus Midheaven is no exception. The difference in focus is that the Taurus Midheaven has learned what security means in a very personal context. Aspects to the Midheaven indicate the "slings and arrows" to which the psyche is subjected; the individual will determines the direction self-knowledge will take. Taurus is a sign that can fool the astrologer. The Taurus Midheaven can persevere through events and circumstances that would completely cow lesser minds. After the worst events have occurred, the Taurus Midheaven may still be ready for another round. By the same token, this individual may stay out of the ring altogether, having learned to fear change and challenge, or having learned that engagement is no longer personally necessary. Either condition is slow to develop and also slow to change.

Tolerance and Trust

The Taurus Midheaven, like the Bull, is actually rather tolerant. This individual is certain of personal beliefs, but does not particularly need to force them on others. On the other extreme, the Taurus Midheaven demands that others adopt Taurean beliefs as the truth without question or exception. Distrust enters when a closely held belief is questioned. Then Taurus Midheavens begin to understand that not everyone shares their rigidly structured beliefs.

For Taurus, to know that he or she is rigid or distrustful could actually provide emotional security. Here, again, the Taurus Midheaven needs space and time to consider every bit of additional self-knowledge. Nowhere is acceptance listed as a basic Taurus trait; it is only through the power of will and devotion that Taurus is able to change.

Desire and Will

The Taurus Midheaven indicates individuals who know the capacity of their own desire and will. Desire is the expression of self on a mundane level; most Taurus Midheavens will express on this level for the most part. Will is the expression of self on the next level of initiation. Thus what appears to be self-informed stubbornness for some will, in others, be expressed as intelligence driven by the impulse of love of a different nature. Another expression of the Taurus Midheaven is either the will to serve self or the will to serve others. Self-serving thoughts are indicative of distorted ego-consciousness; clarity of ego-consciousness allows for one to serve others "with a will."

The esoteric ruler of Taurus is Vulcan. This god forges the hardest of metals in his underground furnaces. When we think of alchemy we are focusing on the dual nature of Taurus as expressed by Vulcan. The alchemists attempted to purify metal, presumably to change lead into gold. Psychologically, the alchemist was attempting to purify the inner essence of self, shedding the dross composed of negative and destructive thoughts, and resolving the stone into a pure expression of one's inner strength. The Taurus Midheaven is often acutely aware of this process and its pitfalls, as well as its ultimate goal.

Resistance

Because resistance is the transition between what exists and what you want to exist, it is apparent that the Taurus Midheaven is resisting the flow of the universe in a particularly powerful way. Taurus says, "I have," but more than that, the Taurus Midheaven says, "I desire to continue to have all that I have now, and to get more." In other words, this type of individual may not be willing to let go of one toy in order to get another.

Human mental capacity is such that the same is true of ideas. The Taurus must allow one idea to move out of consciousness if another is to enter. This movement is directly opposed to the possessiveness of Taurus. So what Taurus can know relates to the way possessiveness functions in his or her life. The distress of displacement may be modified for the Taurus Midheaven when the world is understood as being in a constant state of flux. The goal may be to have understanding above all else. The path focuses on opportunities, not things. The Taurus Midheaven must know this about the self. Nothing is uncreated—it is simply more loosely held.

Neurosis and Sanity

The three thinking styles associated with Taurus at the Midheaven include the following astrological correspondences:

1. The cusp of Aries and Taurus, or the movement from cardinal fire to fixed earth.

2. The pure energy of the fixed earth sign itself.

3. The cusp of Taurus and Gemini, or the movement from fixed earth to mutable air.

These three relationships describe both the neurotic potential of Taurus on the Midheaven and the sanity to be found there.

Aries/Taurus Cusp

The movement from a fire sign to an earth sign is the dynamic of expanded awareness in Buddhist psychology. It involves an overly passionate, emotional reaction to situations and people. There is an intensified territoriality that interferes with meaningful relationship. The opposite expression includes the richness of experience in others, and the capacity to encourage them to share in meaningful ways. If we are holding on too tightly to our own "stuff," we cannot see the richness available for others. When others can see our fullness as well as their own, then the environment thrives.

The feelings of not being or having enough create stinginess with both things and feelings. The higher expression of the same thought is the blinding reality in which physical glamour no longer has power over us. Individuals work out the duality of reality versus perception every day. First they struggle to acquire that which has no permanent value. Then they realize, sometimes too late, that they have held to things that do not matter while never grasping the richness of interpersonal relationships.

As with all the Midheaven signs, a rather small shift of awareness is needed to resolve this neurotic difficulty. The territorial drive is fulfilled by inviting others to be part of it. The potential richness in every situation, by definition, provides enough for everyone. Jesus fed the multitudes with what was perceived to be very little. We all have experiences where the idea was much more comprehensive than the eventual manifestation of it could possibly be. Sharing multiple perceptions of a situation provides deeper understanding than we can achieve alone.

The unconscious skill that assists in this process is the ability to openly explore the territory in a nonjudgmental way. Research has validity only when it is open to any of the possible results. Research takes time. Taurus Midheavens need to allow time for all the facts to come in before they reach a conclusion. They will thus avoid frustration and encourage cooperation from others.

The Pure Energy of Taurus at the Midheaven

The second thinking style of the Taurus Midheaven deals with the energy of the pure fixed earth sign. Resting in the energy of Taurus reflects the pure energy of the earth element as it expresses through the fixed quality. The wisdom of pure Taurus lies in an awareness of the Unity of all things. The steady movement of Taurus, like a plant bursting from the seed and reaching up to the sky, reflects the psychological persistence of the Taurus Midheaven. The positive expression of Taurus at the Midheaven is the direct expression of Unity. In every situation the individual seeks to understand the underlying wholeness that is being expressed.

The neurotic expression of the pure Taurus Midheaven energy involves an ignorance of the true nature of things. If we hold on to this ignorance, we can keep our large homes, our expensive furniture, our quantities of elegant clothes, and all the material things we gather around us to insure our own existence. Security then continues to depend on things that occupy all space in our lives and minds. The sanity of Taurus grows out of dissatisfaction with this accumulation of comfortable things. When a tiny window of awareness opens, Taurus Midheavens glimpse the blinding light of reality. Or perhaps they glimpse the vast void of space, groundless and changeable. Knowing that this is the foundation of unity, one experiences the utter simplicity of true Unity and no longer lives only to acquire and hold on to material wealth. Security lies in knowledge, not in material things.

A profound source of understanding comes from analysis of the process of birth/death/rebirth. The Taurus Midheaven comes to know that there is a component of the present being that continue into the future after death, and that part of one's being has also emerged from the past. The intense physical drama of life and death are seen against the larger background of cycles of lifetimes. From this perspective, grasping becomes silly. This viewpoint can be applied to many of life's situations to good effect. If, on a larger scale, materials things are only temporary, we don't need to invest so much of ourselves in gathering and keeping them. Instead, we can enjoy their true nature while we have them.

Taurus/Gemini Cusp

The third style of Taurus on the Midheaven is concerned with the transition from Taurus to Gemini, or from fixed earth to mutable air. The alchemists used several methods to cause matter to vaporize or to become airy. One was to grind the materia to a fine powder that would "float." The goal was to rise above the material plane to gain perspective. Often we find that effective action is only possible when we can see the larger picture. We no longer have to force a path though every obstacle because we can see ways around our problems.

The neurotic expression of this Taurus Midheaven styles focuses on always acting for personal gain. In Taurus this tendency is magnified at the personal level, causing the individual to seek material wealth in order to repress the sense of powerlessness. For the Taurus Midheaven the tendency to hold on to things even extends to one's neuroses. There would be a sense of loss when a neurosis gives way to sanity. The way toward sanity is to develop a sense of benevolence toward others. When Taurus Midheavens have acquired enough things, they will begin to give them away out of necessity to create physical space for something new. Thus a shift toward sanity is forced upon the individual by the sheer weight of his or her possessions.

An inner source of understanding to counteract this neurotic tendency is the heat of desire. The deep desire for understanding will, through its heat, force spaciousness upon the individual. Then a benevolent view of the world takes hold. Others are not seen as agents for undesirable change. They no longer appear likely to take a valued possession away. Instead they are seen as the source of relationships that are even more valuable. They bring a kind of comfort that is not to be found in solitary maintenance of one's position.

Summary

As the Taurus Midheaven matures, desire for comfort will begin to include spaciousness. The clutter of neurosis will give way to spaciousness in both the physical and the emotional environments. Spiritually, the individual will begin to see the brilliance of simplicity and will share that with others. Less focus on material objects will result in more attention to service as Taurus utilizes personal experience to help others. "I have" will gradually become "I share"—cheerfully, completely, openly. Through this sharing the Taurus Midheaven will have an impact on the world equal to his or her personal desire; this conversion of energy is a powerful force for the change of all humanity.

Conscious Choice

The Taurus Midheaven manifests free will through determined effort. Once decided, a course of action will be followed through to the end. There is a self-awareness of the ability to keep going through difficult as well as rewarding situations. This Midheaven also knows that courage is the key to all effort. Even when the path to one's desires is not clear, courageous effort is still the key, for with determination one can endure events and emerge victorious even when the tasks seem impossible.

The key to ego-consciousness for Taurus is to discern the difference between personal desire and divine will. For the unconscious individual the difference is virtually unidentifiable because both motives are unconscious. For the person who has cultivated self-awareness, personal desire has become a close companion that is well known. Divine will has also revealed itself through a deeper part of the collective mind. This type of will shows with the brilliance of pure light and illuminates everything it touches. The awakened individual can easily act on inspiration that enters consciousness so directly.

Creator/Created—Gaining Self-Knowledge

The creative process for the Taurus Midheaven is synthesis. The individual knows the dualities thoroughly. Human and spiritual longings have made them manifestly clear. The Taurus Midheaven sees that the solution lies in the resolution of polarities, the dissolving of duality into unity. The Taurus Midheaven, at its highest development, permits the individual to know when personal desire is being acted out, as well as when the higher soul's urge is being felt. When these two feelings are merged within consciousness, then no task will be too great for one's creative energy.

Spiritual Awareness

Realization comes for the Taurus when the various dualities begin to merge into expressions of Unity. The individual then knows the nature of Universal Mind and no longer is distracted by false glamour of objects in the world. True realization, however, allows the individual to continue to operate in the world on the human level, interacting with others, teaching and helping them to reach their highest level of enlightenment. The *dharma* of the Taurus Midheaven is to know Unity and to share that knowledge with others gently. One cannot force this knowledge on another. One can only express the knowledge through actions designed to make the truth clearer. The highest realization for Taurus is that each individual will have a unique expression of Unity. This is perhaps the final synthesis for the Taurus Midheaven—to realize that Unity is expressed on the physical plane through the very diversity of experience.

Christine Sizemore

Christine Sizemore is one of the best known multiple personalities on record (chart 12). Her life was the basis of the movie *The Three Faces of Eve*.

With the Moon conjunct the Midheaven, Chris was sensitive from the time she was born. She responded to the world on a deeper psychic level than most people. While the Chris' openness as a child left her open to psychic influences, she was unaware that different personalities were at work, and she was unable to explain herself to the people around her.

Perhaps Chris did not clearly differentiate the ego, memory, and the subconscious until well into her adult life. For her, these three parts of her mind actually blended into each other and, effectively, became one and the same. This is not unusual in small children, but adult self-awareness includes the capacity to store memories as memories, instead of having everything repressed into the unconscious or emerging into consciousness without any control.

The Taurus Midheaven seeks some measure of self-worth. Chris was thrilled that her story would be made into a movie, but was devastated when she did not get to participate personally in the opening. The very act of protecting her withheld the acclaim she needed to bolster her self-esteem. The Taurus Midheaven indicates conscious persistence, as evidenced by her complex course of therapy. Taurus is capable of continuing to work toward a goal long after everyone else has given up and gone home, but Chris did not give up.

Chris saw terrible injuries and deaths in early childhood. She had a deprived childhood and early adult life by most standards, and an abusive first marriage. In spite of all this, she fought to maintain herself psychologically. Her neurotic defenses were elegant and powerful. Her struggle to understand her own psyche was even more courageous. From the depths of the Scorpio IC she was able to draw the power of transformation again and again, and finally was able to become a stable, integrated personality.

On October 19, 1953, Christine experienced the emergence of Jane, the personality whom her therapists saw as an integration of her split personality (the

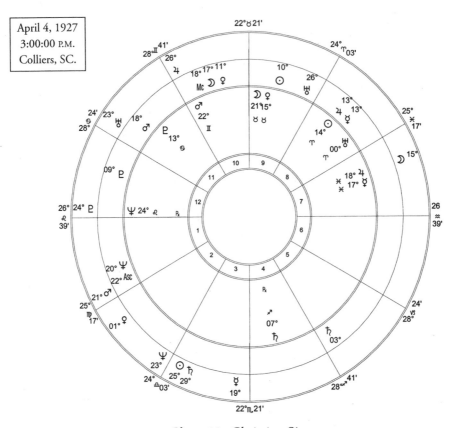

Chart 12. Christine Sizemore

two Eves made famous in the movie). I have focused on the aspects involving the Midheaven and IC and their rulers. Using orbs of one degree, solar arc Jupiter squared Pluto (the attainment of leadership), a strong indicator of the fortunate change that Jane represented. Pluto's involvement suggests the "death" or transformation that needed to occur for Chris to achieve integration. The solar arc Midheaven was square Jupiter, indicating the attainment of success. The solar arc Ascendant trined the Midheaven, indicating that the ego and the self are in balance with each other.

The key to the success was that Chris came to conscious awareness (the Midheaven involvement) of the two battling personalities within herself and caused or allowed a third personality to emerge to resolve the split. Pluto transited to square the Midheaven on September 22, 1952; January 30, 1953; and July 29,

1953; setting the stage for the Scorpio IC to take creative control in some way. Transformation was both essential and inevitable. In addition, transiting Pluto conjuncted Neptune on October 9, 1953, suggesting the intensity of the situation, the critical need for change, and the unusual nature of Chris' psychological problem. Transiting Mars trined the Midheaven on the day Jane emerged, indicating the conditions of readiness for action. While Jane was not the last of Chris' profound psychological changes, it was a strong indication of her will to survive and to achieve self-healing.

Chris' relentless pursuit of wellness has laid the groundwork for revised diagnosis and treatment of multiple personality disorder. Her first doctors thought her disorder was an incurable psychosis, while we now know that the condition is treatable using techniques developed for Chris. She has attained the measure of acclaim that she once so desired completely on the merits of her own strength, as exemplified by the Taurus Midheaven.

Muhammad Ali

Muhammad Ali is an example of a person for whom self-awareness was repressed during childhood (chart 13). "In many ways, as brilliant and charming as he is, Muhammad is an arrested adolescent. There is a lot of pain there. And though he's always tried to put it behind him, shove it out of his mind, a lot of that pain comes from his father, the drinking, the occasional violence, the harangues" (Remnick, p. 85).[1]

At the age of twelve Cassius Clay had his first fight. He said then he would be the greatest. Among the aspects at that time were solar arc Sun squaring and Jupiter semi-squaring the Midheaven, and Pluto conjuncting the Ascendant. Clay knew what he wanted and how to go after it. He was a nutrition nut, didn't drink or smoke. He ran daily and went to the gym. He was not a street fighter. He also refused to play football, because it might ruin his boxing career. By the age of eighteen he was training like a professional. "Ali had the capacity almost of self-hypnosis or self-induced hysteria and he'd work himself up to this crazy pitch." (Remnick, p. 179) He focused on the goal and did not deviate from his path—in true Taurus fashion. He knew what he had to do to be the champ, and he did it to the exclusion of just about everything. He barely graduated from high school. He had to have people read newspaper clippings to him.

---

1. David Remnick, *King of the World: Muhammed Ali and the Rise of an American Hero*. David Remnick (New York: Random House, 1998).

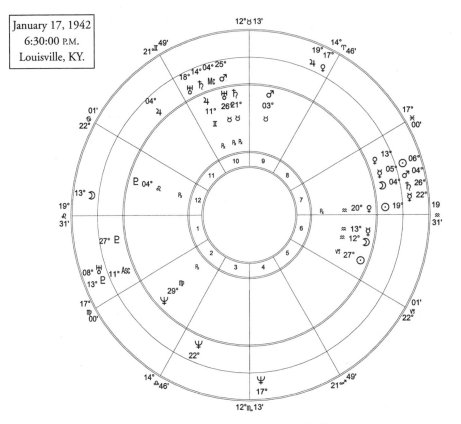

Chart 13. Muhammad Ali

In spite of his intense focus on boxing, Cassius Clay had an eye open to the larger context of his spiritual life. He was attracted to Islam as a teen. He declared his faith after his February 1964 fight with Liston. On March 6, 1964, Elijah Muhammad gave Clay his new name.

Maria Montessori

She enjoyed washing floor tiles and other similar tasks (chart 14). She was sweet, not especially bright, not competitive academically. She found she could do well at school work and became more diligent. She said that once when she was ill, she told her mother, "Don't worry, Mother, I cannot die; I have too much to do" (Kramer, p. 28). As a young child she was bossy, at twelve she became competitive. In the fall of 1883 she entered a technical school.

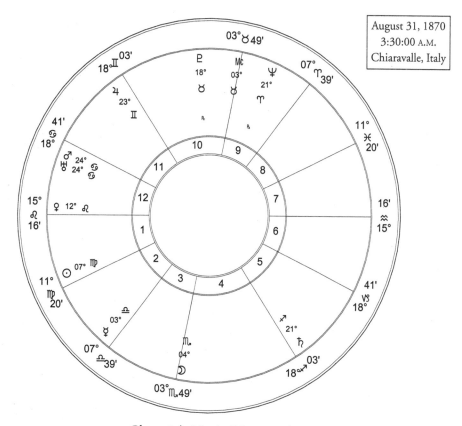

Chart 14. Maria Montessori

"She herself cannot explain how the [mystical experience] happened. She was walking in a street when she passed a woman with a baby holding a long, narrow red strip of paper. I have heard Dr. Montessori describe this little street scene and the decision that then came to her" (Kramer, p. 34).

Maria Montessori summed up her sense of direction by observing that, "We are not born simply to enjoy ourselves . . . [Corals] tiny as they are, can have no outlook beyond their own life. Yet, as a result of their living, new islands and even new continents are born. . . . We human beings, we must have a mission too, of which we are not aware" (Kramer, p. 45). An irony in her life is that Montessori became pregnant by a colleague and had the child. When the father refused to marry her, she gave the child to family members to raise and continued her career of working with children. She said she left her medical career working with mentally deficient children to study education of normal children.

Other Taurus Midheavens

Woody Allen, December 1, 1935, 10:55 P.M., Bronx, New York

Mother Cabrini, July 15, 1850, 7:07 A.M., Lodi, Italy

Edgar Cayce, March 18, 1877, 3:30 P.M., Hopkinsville, Kentucky

Nicolaus Copernicus, February 19, 1473, 4:48 P.M., Torun, Poland

Morgan Fairchild, February 3, 1950, 6:59 P.M., Dallas, Texas

Angela Lansbury, October 16, 1925, 12:45 A.M., London, England

Carl Lewis, July 1, 1961, 7:49 A.M., Birmingham, Alabama

Marilyn Monroe, June 1, 1926, 9:30 A.M., Los Angeles

James Earl Ray, March 10, 1928, 3:00 P.M., Alton, Illinois

Andy Warhol, August 6, 1928, 6:30 A.M., Pittsburgh, Pennsylvania

5

GEMINI MIDHEAVEN

Gemini Midheavens are very nearly square to the Ascendant. This is because Gemini is very close to the solstice point at which a 0-degree Cancer Midheaven would always be mated with a 0-degree Libra Ascendant. The astrological significance of this arrangement is that the individual is neither more Self-directed nor Other-oriented—they show fewer indications of being introverted or extraverted. Such an individual can choose to be introspective or outgoing to a larger degree than most individuals.

This one characteristic connects us immediately to the flexibility of the Gemini Midheaven. Here is an individual who can think through situations and determine how to act. They are responsive to others and often mediate between their own needs and the needs of others. They are less susceptible to guilt, while remaining amenable to persuasion.

Versatility

Gemini Midheavens also know that they are versatile and adaptable. Except in rare situations, the individual can generate choices easily and choose the proper one skillfully. When required to go deeply into one idea or one feeling, this individual may lose track of otherwise simple daily functions, engaging in tunnel vision without being aware of it. They think they can manage everything.

Gemini Midheavens often pursue two or more career paths *at the same time,* trying to do justice to any and all of them. The result may be a scattering of energy and a lack of effective action. However, the result often is a successful management of each and every task which is chosen. The Gemini Midheaven knows how to keep track of many threads in the daily weaving of an interesting fabric of life.

Vigorous Activity

Gemini Midheavens have the capacity to engage in all activities vigorously. If it is worth doing, they think, it is worth doing wholeheartedly. The butterfly may flit from flower to flower, but is fully engaged in this activity.

In terms of typical Western culture, Gemini Midheavens are often rated as a success because they exemplify the thinking mind. Logical processes are second nature to them. In fact, they are certain in the knowledge that they can resolve almost all their problems through the application of logic. Yet, we know that Gemini processes through a less structured, less logical process of moving from one idea to the next. The heart of the process is in movement and not logic.

When an emotional crisis arises, Gemini Midheavens seem to weather it quite well. Yet, we often sense that they have not engaged in the emotional process enough to resolve core issues which are aroused. For example, Gemini Midheavens think through the grieving process when relationships end or when other events occur. They use their thinking skills to manage the situation. Without previous experience of this kind of emotional crisis, they may be unable to get to the bottom of their feelings. Rather than a failure of their thinking process, such a situation is a challenge to broaden the mental and emotional range of choices. After experiencing the uncharacteristic thought processes connected with highly emotional situations, Gemini Midheavens soften their attitudes toward less logical friends and family. As with any of us, they realize the potential strengths and limitations of each mental approach.

With Mercury as the ruler of the Midheaven we find strong mediators in the Gemini Midheaven group. They are skilled negotiators and can be very persuasive. At the same time they can appear to be sly, or even slippery, because they seem to change their tune too easily. I recall from my high school days a slogan which emerged in the Kennedy-Nixon campaign. The Democrats questioned Nixon's integrity by asking, "Would you buy a used car from this man?" Years later, we found that his choices weighed heavily on the side of expediency.

Periodic Creativity

Periods of creativity pepper the lives of Gemini Midheavens. The nature of this energy is to meditate on the future and to mediate in the present. The intuitive function is very strong; for Geminis who have cultivated intuition as well as intellect, the combination is a powerful force for predicting outcomes. They are able to generate a creative idea, mentally project it into the future, and measure the potential outcomes.

The creative process is enhanced because they are capable of objective thought. They are able to perceive the broad landscape as well as the individual flower. The Gemini Midheaven knows about the capacity to think about an idea, to measure it in physical terms, to simulate reality at the thinking level before a product is manifested in physical reality. They may not be as adept at implementing ideas on a practical level, but they "know" how something will work. They know because they have used mind to imagine the product in the world; they have seen it work with the mind's eye.

Impermanence

Gemini Midheavens understand that impermanence is the nature of the world. A useful slogan for them is "It just doesn't matter," because in terms of cosmic time, not much will have lasting importance. This attitude sometimes seems superficial—on the spiritual level it has the exactitude which accompanies all profound truths.

There is a fundamentally different sense of ownership and control which frees the Gemini to entertain ideas of change. These individuals know that they have the use of objects in the world, of relationships, even of ideas, but only for some finite period of time. It is this very understanding of impermanence that provides Gemini Midheavens with the self-awareness to manage resourcefully. If you only have something for a limited time, make the best of it while you have it. Wisdom comes with the knowledge to avoid flippant or wasteful processes.

Diversity

The Gemini Midheaven cultivates ego-consciousness concerning diversity. These individuals are able to identify with individual differences which enrich human interaction. They acknowledge and recognize traits which may not occupy significant positions in their own consciousness. They encourage others to pursue what is personally significant, rather than laying out a set of rules which others must follow. (In the following discussion of neurosis we can see that the Gemini Midheaven does not always engage in this kind of open-minded relationship. Still, it is an ever-present beacon which guides one toward right action in relationships.)

Geminis have diverse personal interests as well. They may put together a set of interests and skills which appears to be random and nonsensical, yet they cultivate an ego-consciousness which relishes the variety. Perhaps more than any other sign on the Midheaven, Gemini knows when it is time to move on to the next job, the next date, or the next idea.

Resistance

Resistance is the temporal transition between what exists and what one wants to exist. Resistance is a psychological function which the Gemini Midheaven can understand as thoroughly as they understand the thought processes. Gemini, as a mutable sign, is less apt to become caught in resistance. Yet, they will be fully aware of it when it happens. They will become frustrated with their own inability to overcome it, particularly if they have been able to move through difficult periods of their life with relative ease.

Because Gemini people are such skillful mediators, they often can mediate between their own opposing thoughts, desires, and feelings. Far from being thoughtless, they are capable of intensely focused mental process. They resist the very idea of being resistant. They like to believe that they are flexible and adaptable in all things. This contrasts with Aquarius, who also has the depth of thought, or any other fixed sign, whose focus may be on holding on more than on changing.

Capacity To Respond

A troubled Gemini Midheaven will identify the tendency to react instead of responding to situations. This will be considered a flaw in the thought process, if not actually a character flaw. Gemini Midheavens know they are good in emergencies *because* they can respond in a flexible manner. When they experience periods of nonresponsive (reactive) behavior, they know they have lost something precious. The adaptable Gemini has been critical of others who are less able to manage their difficulties—now that criticism comes back to haunt them.

The flip side of such a condition is that Geminis learn from each and every experience, constantly broadening their base of choice-making behaviors. Thus they truly *are* more flexible, more adaptable, more capable. The basic skill is the ability to get through the rapids without tipping over the boat. Geminis may depend on others to make repairs when they reach calmer waters. When they get to the difficult moment, they know enough about themselves to recognize the need to be in the moment and to take effective action.

Sanity and Neurosis

The three thinking styles associated with Gemini at the Midheaven include the following astrological correspondences:

1. The cusp of Taurus and Gemini, or the movement from fixed earth to mutable air

2. The pure energy of the mutable air sign itself

3. The cusp of Gemini and Cancer, or the movement from mutable air to cardinal water.

These three relationships describe both the neurotic potential of Gemini on the Midheaven and the sanity to be found there.

Taurus / Gemini Cusp

The movement from an earth sign to an air sign is the dynamic of effective action in Buddhist psychology. The movement from fixed earth to mutable air is the transition from comfortable, grounded perceptions to an objectivity based on the appreciation of change. Where the Aquarian Midheaven focuses on the doubt of permanence, the Gemini Midheaven is more worried about the possibility that change itself will cease. Alchemically the movement from earth to air involves rising up to gain objectivity, then sinking down to test an idea in its solid form. The very movement of change becomes a constant for Gemini, a barometer of the appropriateness of situations. When movement stops, problems begin for the Gemini Midheaven. Even the appearance of slowing down the pace is not appealing to them. The lack of movement is seen as a slowing of life processes in some way, a diminishing of personal power.

The sanity of this profound relationship to change lies in the fact that nothing is permanent, everything changes. To be aware of this truth is to align oneself with the cosmos. Then the Gemini Midheaven can learn the nuances of pacing. Sometimes change is like the subtle breeze through the leaves of a tree on a hot summer day; sometimes it is like a hurricane destroying everything in its path. Gemini Midheavens can cultivate an appreciation for a full range of change.

The Pure Energy of Gemini at the Midheaven

The second thinking style of the Gemini Midheaven involves the energy of the pure mutable fire sign. Resting in the energy of Gemini reflects the pure energy of the air element as it expresses through the mutable quality. Gemini Midheavens require space the same way that air is required to breathe. The Aquarian is more comfortable with contained space, while the Gemini wants as much openness as possible.

Neurosis becomes evident when the Gemini demands space where structure would serve better. The Gemini Midheaven is more likely to feel claustrophobia than any other sign. The desire for space in which to operate is closely connected with the desire for flexibility of choice. The decision-making process, for Gemini, requires mental space. The Gemini Midheaven knows this and therefore structures all of life to accommodate this requirement. Meditation can bring the sense of spaciousness into every activity. Then the apparent structure of situations and events is seen as the temporary illusion it really is.

Gemini / Cancer Cusp

The third thinking style of the Gemini Midheaven is concerned with the transition from Gemini to Cancer, or from mutable air to cardinal water. In alchemy the relationship of air and water reflects the need for breathing to sustain human life. On the physical level we are able to dip into the water, but we cannot live there without air. On the psychic level the metaphor of air and water describes the movement between intellect and intuition in Buddhist psychology. When Gemini get stuck in either intellect or intuition, pain is the result. For Gemini sanity lies in the capacity to move between these states of mind. The Gemini Midheaven becomes rigid and inflexible when movement is prevented. Both intellect and intuition are needed for effective action; understanding the spaciousness of reality helps to maintain or restore movement between them.

Conscious Choice

It is hard on the rest of the world when Gemini Midheavens decide they know what is best and then demand it. The typical Gemini is easygoing, doing what he or she wants without much desire to influence others. When Gemini tries to coerce others, it is with a barrage of words which have some logic but have no feeling. The logic is designed to dictate behavior and thought of others. This energy is difficult to resist because it is like a wind—nothing is there, exactly, yet we feel the force.

Gemini Midheavens can engage free will to go their own way with a minimum of fuss. They generally do not cause problems for others except that they change direction rather frequently. It's just that Gemini wants us to go along for the fun as well as to contribute effort or money to the situation. The more enlightened Gemini Midheavens knows that they must come up with the resources to complete each project. The more enlightened Gemini Midheaven leaves fewer and fewer messes behind as they go through life.

Spiritual Awareness

When the Gemini Midheaven slows down and rests, then meditative practice helps to train the mind. The sheer force of mental activity can be directed into contemplative practice, but not as easily as for, say, a Taurus. Gemini Midheavens can make good use of movement practices which bring the mind into the body on a moment to moment basis. This will help them to connect to the karma-mental processes and will lend a tone of reality to their actions.

Because Gemini does not feel like the source but rather is more process-oriented, it may be harder for these individuals to identify with unity. However, once they grasp the essential knowledge of impermanence, they are perfectly capable of acting as though things are permanent for the duration of time when those things are in their lives. Then they can let go of the old and move on, relatively unencumbered by old business. Thus, Gemini's existence is lightened materially as well as enlightened spiritually.

Mozart and Madonna

In childhood Mozart was reported to be a sweet child who accepted his life as a performer and followed his father's directions in all things (chart 15). By doing this, he was the financial support of his entire family. Biographers indicate that his childhood was very one-sided. "From the moment he discovered music, his interest in every other occupation was as dead, and even children's games had to have a musical accompaniment if they were to interest him" (Solomon, p. 13). Mozart's music exemplifies a delicately balanced tension between form and disorder, a precarious negotiation of the fragile borders that separate the familiar from the alien. He diverged from the traditional pure melodies and colors, adding "a tinge of strangeness to the beautiful" (Solomon, p. 373).

As he approached puberty, he changed, developing a mind of his own. But because of the lopsided childhood of performance-driven activities, Mozart never

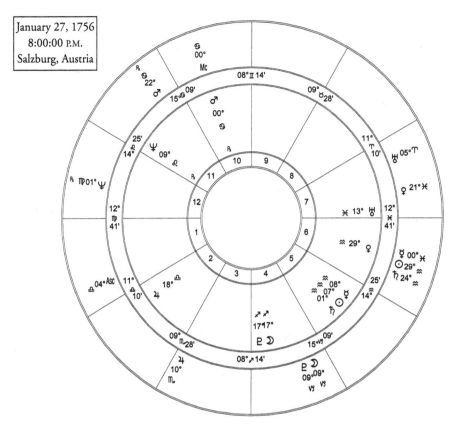

Chart 15. Mozart

was able to manage his instinctual desires, and thus was subject to them as a phys-ical driving force. The fire in the Sagittarius IC erupted at puberty as a sexual impulse and lack of verbal or any other kind of moderation. Whatever structure his life had in childhood was overthrown.

Beginning in mid-1775, with solar arc Jupiter (ruler of the IC) quincunx the Midheaven (desire to be important), the solar arc Moon (changing life objectives), and Pluto (recklessness) formed the same aspect in April of 1776. In November of that year the solar arc Midheaven trined Venus (self-admiration) and shortly thereafter Mozart fell in love with Aloysia (sister of his Constanza, whom he mar-ried in 1782). In late 1777 the solar arc Midheaven conjuncted Mars (excitable disposition) and two months later Mercury (ruler of the Midheaven) trined Mars (tendency to rashness and exaggeration). In July of 1779, when the Midheaven formed a quincunx to Saturn (indicating career difficulties), Mozart was well on

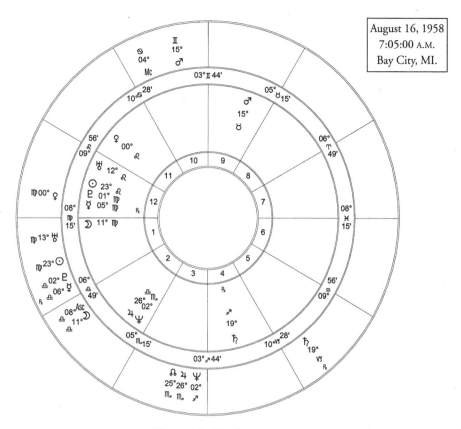

August 16, 1958
7:05:00 A.M.
Bay City, MI.

Chart 16. Madonna

his way to acting out all his unfulfilled childhood possibilities, but without the benefit of any practical experience, refinement, or structure.

There is no denying Mozart's musical genius. If he had experienced anything like a normal childhood, he would have been better prepared to deal with the stresses of puberty, and he might have entered his adult life with greater philosophical grounding and some practical instruction about how to manage his career. Instead, he rebelled against his father's restrictions and proceeded to make a mess of his personal and professional life.

Madonna provides an interesting contrast to Mozart (chart 16). Her management of her career and finances is far more skillful. She has a wonderful voice and uses it well. She has a background in ballet, modern and jazz dance, and learned to play drums, guitar, and keyboards. She is extreme—in appearance, in her dress, in her performance. From Marilyn Monroe blond to black leather, she demonstrates the ability to use her talents as an actress to further her musical career. She plays the extremes for effect in a market that is all about extremes.

In the natal chart Mercury squares the Midheaven (career advancement through the pursuit of defined goals), Venus sextiles the Midheaven (the opportunity to find love), and Pluto squares the Midheaven (capacity to exert power). She also has Saturn 165 degrees from the Midheaven (a similar compulsion to Mozart's, through which she studied and practiced a range of artistic modes, whereas he focused on only one). The quincunx to Neptune suggests the capacity to adjust her image to suit the market.

She starred in *Dick Tracy* in 1990. While some reviewers didn't like this film, it was a four-star hit and represented her success as an actress as well as a musician. During the period of filming Madonna's solar arc Midheaven was trining natal Neptune (the capacity to put on an act). At the time it was released, she had solar arc Midheaven sextile Mercury (career advancement), solar arc Neptune opposition the Midheaven (awareness of the "act" in the world), and solar arc Pluto trine the Midheaven (achieving recognition and greater independence).

It is interesting to note that in 1990 Madonna also met with Disney executives to discuss a possible role as Evita.[1] This movie did not begin filming until 1996 and was released in December of that year.

At age forty-one Madonna has already outlived Mozart by six years and shows no signs of ending her multifaceted performance career.

Tiger Woods

This phenomenal golf player was into the game as soon as he could stand up (chart 17). He loved watching his father practice, and he was a natural golfer from the time he could walk. By age two he was practicing swings, and even knew the names for them. At the age of three he shot a score of forty-eight for nine holes. And this was not a case of his father pushing him into the game— Tiger wanted it himself. Before he was five years old, he had a professional golf teacher.

Yet Tiger is a well-liked, courteous person who took his education seriously and who developed the kind of character his parents had in mind. One of his worst rounds of golf was played on the day his father was hospitalized for chest pains associated with a bronchial problem. Tiger did not play well, but also did not complain. His playing partner, John Cook, said, "He showed me a lot today,

---

1. www.execpc.com/~reva/html/7f.htm

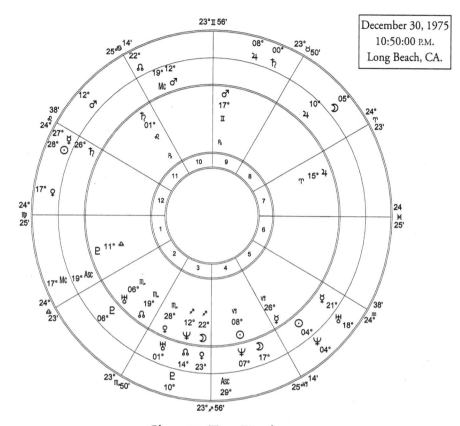

23°♊56'

December 30, 1975
10:50:00 P.M.
Long Beach, CA.

Chart 17. Tiger Woods

and it wasn't golf. You can lose your mind out there and he didn't. . . . He just tried to fight through it" (Teague, p. 64).

Astrologically, Tiger Woods demonstrates the alchemical partnership of air and water. He has deep emotional ties to his family and to his beliefs. At the same time he has the intellectual strength to focus his mind on his goals and work toward them. The important key to this type of Gemini Midheaven is the movement between the two. Tiger uses both to his advantage in golf and in other areas of his life. On the day when he played so badly because of worry about his father, solar arc Saturn was approaching a sextile to his Midheaven, and the solar arc Midheaven formed a very close square to his Jupiter, ruler of the fourth house of family. It is clear that he has his priorities straight in his life.

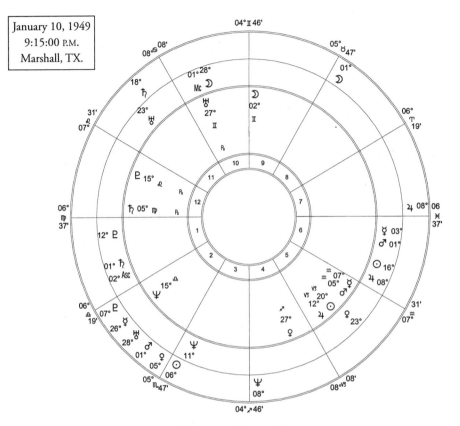

Chart 18. George Foreman

George Foreman

George Foreman made boxing history by reclaiming the heavyweight title at forty-five years of age (chart 18).[2] In 1974 he lost it to Muhammad Ali by a knockout, and twenty years later he reclaimed the title, again by a knockout.

Foreman was regarded as invincible after he defeated Joe Frazier with a devastating knockout. He was supremely confident when he met Muhammad Ali, expecting a usual early knockout. Instead Ali frustrated him with the "rope-a-dope" strategy, taking many of Foreman's best punches on his arms while barely avoiding bombs to the head. Eventually Foreman became fatigued and Ali was able to win. Foreman could not accept the defeat and lost the will to fight. He later lost to Jimmy Ellis and announced an early retirement.

---

2. "Foreman Drops Moorer in Tenth," Boulder *Sunday Camera*, November 6, 1994.

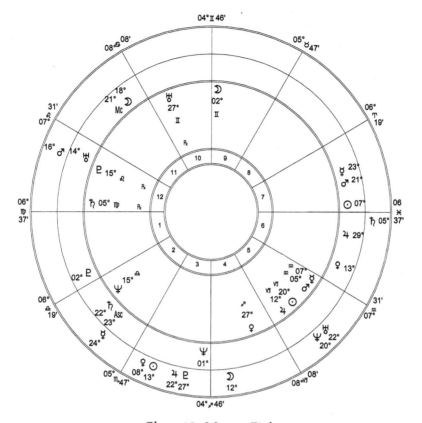

Chart 19. Moorer Fight

Foreman's persona changed. Often sullen and menacing, he became an ordained minister and evolved a jovial, paternal exterior. But he could not forget the defeat in the ring. Long after what should have been his prime, the overweight Foreman began a comeback that culminated in his surprising knockout of Michael Moorer. He thus became the oldest man (by five years) to win a professional boxing championship. At the weigh-in for the fight, Foreman is quoted as saying, "I might have to break the sixth commandment." A brutal man in a brutal sport, it is all the more remarkable that he accomplished the feat while being accepted as a lovable, self-effacing country preacher. Foreman proved himself a master of public relations, matched only by his nemesis, Muhammad Ali.

While there are numerous aspects by transit and solar arc for each fight, those to the Midheaven are significant by themselves. For the Ali fight, George Foreman has solar arc Midheaven past a sextile to the North Node and past a semi-square to Pluto. It seems that the tension that marks peak performance may have passed by the day of the fight. Mercury applied to square the Midheaven. Ebertin identifies this aspect as "vocational changes." Transiting Saturn formed a semi-square to the Midheaven, indicating hindered progress and difficulties in one's occupation.

For the Moorer fight George had solar arc Midheaven past a quincunx to the Sun and applying to semi-square the Ascendant (chart 19). The solar arc Midheaven was midway between the natal Midheaven and Ascendant, indicating a time when he was capable of experiencing a strong alignment of what he knew about himself and what he showed to the world. Without supporting aspects this might have meant little. However, the solar arc Moon formed a semi-square to the Midheaven and solar arc Mars made a semi-square to Mercury, the ruler of the Midheaven. His objectives were deeply felt at the soul level, and he was able to achieve his goals through a powerful determination. Without the spiritual and physical focus, this fight would have been a reckless venture for a man his age. As it turned out, he made an impressive statement indeed about his ability as a fighter.

Other Gemini Midheavens

Patty Hearst, February 20, 1954, 6:01 P.M., San Francisco, California

Ernest Hemingway, July 21, 1899, 8:00 A.M., Oak Park, Illinois

John Keats, October 29, 1795, 1:30 A.M., London, England

George Bush, June 12, 1924, 11:30 A.M., Milton, Massachusetts

Doris Day, April 3, 1922, 4:30 P.M., Cincinnati, Ohio

Ignatius Loyola, December 24, 1491, 10:00 P.M., Azpeitia, Spain

Howard Hughes, December 24, 1905, 11:00 P.M., Houston, Texas

Anaïs Nin, February 21, 1903, 8:30 P.M., Neuilly, France

Walter Koch, September 18, 1895, 6:25 A.M., Esslingen, Germany

Warren Beatty, March 30, 1937, 5:30 P.M., Richmond, Virginia

Hank Aaron, February 5, 1934, 8:45 P.M., Mobile, Alabama

6

CANCER MIDHEAVEN

When the Midheaven is in Cancer, the Ascendant is very nearly 90 degrees away. The angle between the Midheaven and Ascendant is similar to Gemini, but tending to move in the opposite direction, as the Midheaven is on the opposite side of the solstice point at 0 degrees Cancer. In the Northern Hemisphere the range is from 84 to 95 degrees, while in the Southern Hemisphere the range is from 90 to 121 degrees.

The closer the angle is to 90 degrees, the more we see the assertive nature of this cardinal water sign revealed. The balance between self-direction and responsiveness to others is affected by the placements of the planets in eastern and western halves of the chart, but starts from a broadbased capacity of choice. Cancer Midheavens know themselves to be planners, capable of organizing and directing their lives and the activities of others as well. This self-awareness accompanies a consideration for others and reserves independence for the self. It includes the capacity to nurture self and other in a simple, conservative manner. These seemingly incompatible traits are woven into an elegant unit for the Cancer Midheaven.

Conscious of Individuality

Cancer Midheavens are aware of their own individuality. They can appreciate the importance of individual differences and support them consistently. Because Cancer focuses on the ability to change in a smooth, flowing manner, they know from deep within themselves how to allow processes to unfold without undue interference. Cancer Midheavens nurture individuality in themselves and others. They expect others to allow them the same opportunities as a matter of course.

Sensitivity and Impressionability

The nature of flowing material is to conform to the shape of the container. Water fills a glass; water flows over and around rocks in a stream, taking on the shape of the hillside. Similarly, Cancer Midheavens are aware of their sensitivity to the thoughts and emotions found in their surroundings. They are able to perceive the flow and shift their energies on subtle levels of mind and body. As such, Cancer Midheavens are impressionable, subject to influence. Think of the crab. On land he moves under his own power, but in a strong current of water the water pulls him along and he is assaulted by sand, seaweed, or whatever else is carried in the current.

   The crab has a hard shell. The force of the current does not disintegrate him. Even when he is carried a long distance, he remains himself. The same is true of Cancer Midheavens. Pushed by intense emotional energies, they retain their intrinsic sense of self. As individuals they have been affected by outside forces, but they retain self-awareness of their separation from others. Like the crab, they allow the flow to touch them, even to persuade them, with relatively little internal change.

Independence

The shell of the crab is a home that he carries with him everywhere. Cancer Midheavens have a shell of sorts, a contained sense of self that is always with them. Mythology includes beings known as shapeshifters. They are people who can take on the form of animals or even trees. Zeus took on the form of animals in many stories about his conquests. The planet Jupiter is exalted in Cancer—the ability to change shape consciously to suit conditions is an example of Jupiter's expansive abilities reflected in the Cancer Midheaven.

   Cancer Midheavens can assume an appearance of thoughts and feelings to suit their circumstances, just as the crab can float on the tide or walk on the sand.

Cancer Midheavens remain essentially the same, changed only as much as they choose to be changed. This ability to shift in appearance serves Cancer Midheavens by allowing them to fit into situations with relative ease. Even if they are intensely uncomfortable about events, they can appear to go along with the flow. Later people can be shocked to find that they have not been permanently swayed at all. A look at the Cancer Midheaven charts shows us that they have the ability to pursue goals *and* to become popular at the same time. Napoleon did not become a great general by making enemies of his troops; Elizabeth Taylor's acting career depended on pleasing others. Both had irrepressible personalities.

Consideration for Others

It is the devotion of Neptune, the esoteric ruler of Cancer, that reflects the ability of the Cancer Midheaven to show consideration. The Moon's influence allows them to feel what others are feeling and Neptune reflects what they do about those feelings. No one is uniformly considerate of everyone. Still, the Cancer Midheavens I know are certainly able to demonstrate that they care about others and wish them well. This occurs from the level of a teenager who is generally friendly and never acts spitefully, to the level of the individual who has taken *Boddhisattva* vows and devoted her life to helping others through hospice work. In between we find people who have favorite charities or other activities that demonstrate their concern for others.

Thrift

Ebertin (p. 86) mentions thrift as a Cancer Midheaven quality. When I think of Elizabeth Taylor's ability to spend, I wonder where thrift fits into the picture. In the Cancer Midheavens I know personally, one is definitely a saver, though he avoids the miser label. Another is able to make something out of apparent nothing time and time again. A third established a business in a very limited market. These examples provide a sense of the range of management capacity. Cancer Midheavens can fall anywhere in the range from miser to spendthrift. Even Elizabeth Taylor's spending is seldom reckless, considering how much money she has.

Simplicity

The simplicity of a quiet meditation space exemplifies the Cancer Midheaven. These individuals provide for themselves, in whatever form, a physical or mental space where there is calm and where the energies of life can be allowed to meander like an old river. One Cancer Midheaven I know has an apartment full of antique furniture (not terribly expensive). There is a unified feeling to the space that spells simplicity and encourages calm.

Nurturing Capacity

Cancer Midheavens are aware of their capacity to nurture others. While a Cancer Sun might nurture in a natural, less self-conscious way, the Cancer Midheaven knows the depth of this side of the psyche. Pearl Buck won a Nobel Prize for *The Good Earth*, a story about a Chinese family. She drew on her own sense of family and nurturing to write this book. Elizabeth Taylor, famous for her movies and infamous for her many marriages, constantly traveled with her own children and those she adopted. She made time for all of them in spite of her hectic career.

Cancer Midheavens have a conscious relationship with food. They also realize the value of other forms of nurturing. These individuals can provide emotional and spiritual support as well as physical sustenance. They understand the developmental processes involved on all levels of the psyche and their need for support.

Resistance

Resistance occupies the space between what one currently has and what one wants. For Cancer Midheavens this resistance relates to the container in many ways. Individuals define their own container. The outside world may have definite ideas about the nature of the container but they can influence it very little. When Cancer Midheavens wish to experience change, they usually flow with the tide, and wait for the tide to flow in the desired direction. Resistance becomes a problem when the tide goes the wrong way. The crab fights for what it wants, occasionally losing a claw in the process.

Cancer Midheavens, like the crab, can grow new claws. We can never count them out because of this capacity for self-renewal. They know that seemingly devastating blows to their ego, their career, and their families can be healed with time and effort. Like the shapeshifter, they change to accommodate circumstances, regrowing their inner emotional resources for another day.

Capacity to Respond

Because they can pour themselves into activities, Cancer Midheavens have the capacity to respond to whatever situations arise. They can also choose not to respond, remaining self-contained and apparently uncaring. One risk is that the container will become closed and rigid, in which case no visible response can be seen. In these conditions the internal turmoil may be intense, rather like a pressure cooker. Occasionally the lid will fly off, releasing the pressure in a destructive manner. Cancer Midheavens use what they know about themselves to avoid such a calamity, developing emotional and intellectual release valves to protect themselves. In situations that demand response, these valves can open and close, maintaining a sense of individual self while responding sympathetically to others.

Sanity and Neurosis

The three thinking styles associated with Cancer at the Midheaven include the following astrological correspondences:

1. The cusp of Gemini and Cancer, or the movement from cardinal water to fixed fire.

2. The pure energy of the cardinal water sign itself.

3. The cusp of Cancer and Leo, or the movement from cardinal water to fixed fire.

These three relationships describe both the neurotic potential of Cancer on the Midheaven and the sanity to be found there.

Gemini/Cancer Cusp

The movement from an air sign to a water sign is the dynamic of rain falling. If it is a gentle rain, it nurtures the earth by supplying plants with the moisture they need and by washing away whatever debris has collected on the ground. On the other hand, if it is a major thunderstorm, it washes away the topsoil, pulls plants up by the roots, and causes raging floods. Something similar happens with this first expression of the sanity and neurosis of the Cancer Midheaven. The usual calm demeanor that flows along can become angry and destructive. Then clarity is lost in the rage and confusion.

Between calmness and rage are many degrees of possibility. Cancer Midheavens master many areas of their emotional lives but occasionally reveal one or another emotional storm. The sanity that balances this neurosis is like the clarity that is produced in mountain lakes in calm weather. We know the lake is deeper than we can see, yet the surface reflects the sky perfectly. This clarity is the result, for Cancer Midheavens, of the merging of intellect and feeling. The resulting calm provides the basis for all action in their lives.

The Pure Energy of Cancer at the Midheaven

The second thinking style of Cancer involves the energy of the pure cardinal water sign. Resting in the energy of Cancer reflects the pure energy of the water element as it expresses through the cardinal quality. Cancer Midheavens sit still and perceive the nature of their minds. One sinks if one remains still in water. Unable to breathe, there is a feeling of pressure that comes from unconscious contents of the mind that press to become conscious. There is a fear of being overwhelmed by such a rush of feelings, like being caught in flood. To avoid the fear, the Cancer Midheaven may ignore the flood, which is a very dangerous tactic.

By contrast, the sanity of this thinking style lies in the ability to imagine the spaciousness of the ocean and to imagine being part of it. The ocean provides a space in which to experience emotions, like the air provides space for thought. Sanity arises because the ocean allows emotions to be expressed and to dissipate, instead of being solidified. This allows Cancer Midheavens to own their feelings but not be attached to them. They sink to a point and then are able to resurface.

Cancer/Leo Cusp

The third thinking style of the Cancer Midheaven is concerned with the transition from Cancer to Leo, or from cardinal water to fixed fire. In the heat of summer the sign of Cancer gives way to Leo, the hot period of summer when plants gain maturity. If there is not enough water, everything withers and dies in the heat. If there is too much rain, plants cannot mature properly, and never bear fruit. The desired state is a balance of both water and heat. Sanity here is in the balance between feelings and intuition. Neurosis expresses through imbalance of these expressions.

With too much heat there is a consuming desire which grasps at things that are intended to satisfy the emotions. Rather than satisfaction, however, one does not appreciate them, but discards them in order to grasp something else. The fire seduces one into a repetitive cycle of getting and discarding. In such a cycle very little creativity can manifest. This behavior prevents closeness with others and magnifies feelings of isolation. The more isolated one feels, the more one tries to counteract the feeling by grasping both people and things.

Balance between water and fire, for the Cancer Midheaven, creates an environment in which feelings can be expressed and acknowledged. Feelings of isolation give way to enjoyment of the spaciousness of awareness. This awareness includes an accommodation of other people, particularly loved ones; it also allows for awareness of the intrinsic value of things as themselves. Instead of grasping at people and things to provide emotional security, Cancer Midheavens develop a style of sharing and nurturing without so much internal tension.

Summary

It is the nature of water to flow downhill and to fill the container. This cardinal water sign has the ability to identify and place the container first, and then let the water flow into it. Fast or slow, calm or roiling, Cancer's energy continues to flow to the predetermined container. This relentless flow of energy is what allows Cancer on the Midheaven to fulfill goals. Don't mistake the downhill flow as a negative direction. Cancer uses the drive of feeling energy in a very positive way—decision and action are charged by personal judgment and driven by gut feelings that this Midheaven learns to trust implicitly.

Creativity

Creative flow is important for Cancer Midheavens. They do not have bursts of creativity as much as they have a steady rhythm to their work. If that pattern becomes dammed up by emotions or thoughts, they experience an uncharacteristic blockage that can be quite painful. This is like the moment before the tide turns. In this case there is no movement to be seen. Three remedies are available. First, there can be an earthquake in the psyche that destroys the dam. This could occur in an emergency situation that pushes Cancer Midheavens beyond the obstacle. Second, the Cancer Midheaven could systematically whittle away at the dam of emotions until no obstacle remains. Third, through a process of seepage the creative process could circumvent the obstacle. While systematically removing the obstacle seems the best choice, the others actually will work well in certain situations. All three are useful approaches to the problem of blocked creativity.

Conscious Choice

The metaphors for creativity are also metaphors for the use of free will. Cancer Midheavens know that they can not only be in the flow, they can create it. Like water being pushed upward in an artesian spring, inspiration arises from deep within the self. A significant part of that inner spring is will and the power to make things happen. The energy of devotion drives Cancer Midheavens and they know how to direct the devoted will effectively. The will can be blocked for a time; it can be the tool that erodes the dam eventually, and will to express the self can get around massive obstacles, leaving them where they stand. Cancer Midheavens can flow around you, leaving you high and dry like an island amid their activity, or they can sweep you away in a flood of energy. Both are expressions of Cancer Midheaven's will.

Spiritual Growth

Once again, the metaphors for creativity can be used to describe the enlightenment process. Whatever life experiences crop up on the path of Cancer Midheavens, they offer greater self-awareness. When one becomes aware of an insurmountable obstacle and changes one's path, that is conscious awareness. When an earthquake of inner illumination occurs, there is enlightenment. When the truth seeps into awareness bit by bit, that also is realization. For Cancer Midheavens, knowledge comes through devotion to the search, as well as through an opening of the inner being to knowledge. When both of these happen, then spiritual growth occurs.

Colette

Sidonie Gabrielle Colette was perhaps the most famous female French author of her day (chart 20).[1] Her deep insight into the psychology of her characters was paired with vivid images to produce stories filled with sexual impact. Her first husband published her work under his name and pretended to be her collaborator, but she was the inspiration behind the early work and all that came after. In addition to erotically rich novels, Colette also wrote from her childhood experiences. *Gigi*, one of her later works (1944–45), inspired a movie by that name.

Colette's Cancer Midheaven forms a biquintile to the Sun, indicating the creative talent that emerges from her childhood experience (Sun in the fourth house). The trine to Mars suggests the drive to achieve success. The quintile to Neptune in the seventh indicates both the influence of her marriages and sexual affairs on her writing, and the ability to spark the imagination through her writing. The Midheaven squaring the Ascendant indicates a balanced sense of self, as shown by her ability to respond to others and to stand on her own. With Venus

1. Information about Colette was gathered from the CD-Rom version of *Grolier's Encyclopedia*, and from memory.

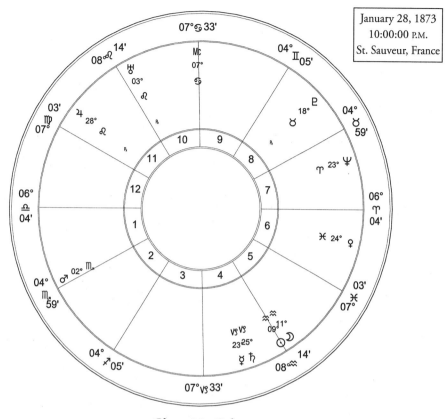

Chart 20. Colette

biseptile and Jupiter septile the Midheaven, there is a hint of fate in the unfolding of Colette's career. If she had been born today, for example, her husband would not have found it easy to claim her novels as his own.

Sir Isaac Newton

Isaac Newton was born prematurely (chart 21).[2] He was very nearsighted, but never obtained glasses. He was not a good student at first, but when he was challenged by another student, he became intensely competitive at his studies.

In 1665 Newton left Cambridge for two years because of the plague. During these years he developed the basis of integral calculus several years before it was independently discovered by Leibniz. He did this by gathering bits and pieces of separate theories. While Newton did not develop the logical proofs for calculus,

---

2. D. C. Ipsen, *Isaac Newton, Reluctant Genius* (Nillside: Enslow, 1985).

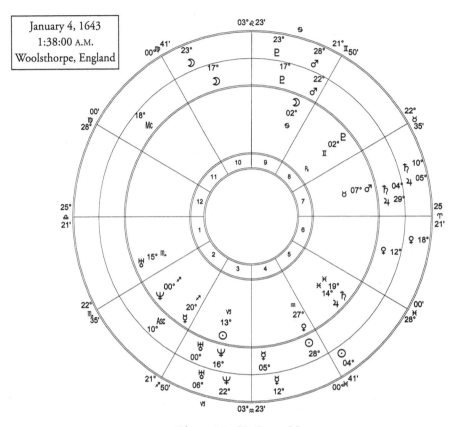

Chart 21. Sir Isaac Newton

he is credited with the development of problem-solving tools for mathematical analysis.

In 1683 his treatise *Principia* was published. Often called the greatest scientific book ever written, this work analyzed the motions of bodies in various media under the action of centripetal forces. The results, when applied to orbiting bodies in conjunction with the law of gravity, provide the basis for modern astronomy.

In 1693 Newton became very ill—mercury poisoning from his chemical experiments was suspected. However, at about the same time a fire destroyed many of his writings, and some thought he went into a deep depression as a result.

Newton's birth time varies depending on the source. *AstroDatabank* indicates a rectified time of 1:38 A.M., while Marc Penfield quotes 1:00 A.M. Using the year of Newton's severe depression after a fire destroyed his written work, I arrived at a rectified birth time of 12:51 A.M. Rectification using the Midheaven is best done by using events involving changes in status and career, or that indicate changes in one's state of mind—the fire and subsequent mental illness serve both functions. This chart shows Pluto conjunct the Midheaven by solar arc, solar arc Ascendant sesqui-square the Midheaven, and solar arc Midheaven sextile Uranus. Solar arc Pluto conjuncting the Midheaven confirms that an outside agent is involved (the fire), and that Newton felt his power threatened. In a very real sense the fire could have ruined his career. The Ascendant-Midheaven aspect focuses on the relationship between the ego and the personality. Uranus-Midheaven aspects indicate sudden events (the fire). At this time solar arc Venus opposed the Ascendant, suggesting disharmony and wastefulness (Newton was unable to continue his work because of the illness).

The Midheaven in Newton's natal chart reflects the need for balance between water and fire signs. In most people's lives, there would be no actual fire, but in Newton's case the fire is the agent that caused him to enter a deep depression (some called this a nervous breakdown). After this illness, Newton retired from scientific research, and sought a government position. The conjunction of Pluto to the Midheaven thus indicated a change of career—he became warden of the royal mint, and was made its master in 1699. This powerful position allowed him significant earnings and led to his later knighthood.

None of my readings indicated that Newton was a nurturing type of person. Although he may not have nurtured other people, he did cultivate both his scientific and his government careers.

John Lennon

John Lennon was a cultural and music icon who has inspired musicians since he burst on the musical scene in the United States with the Beatles (chart 22).[3] "Lennon was capable of inspired, brutally honest confessional songwriting and melodic song craft. But the extremes, both in his music and his life, were what made him fascinating . . . Lennon dabbled in everything from revolutionary politics to the television talk-show circuit during the early '70s" (Erlewine, *All Music Guide*).

Two birth times are suggested for John Lennon. Marc Penfield lists 7:00 A.M. while *AstroDatabank* indicates a time of 6:30 p.m. The 7:00 P.M. time gives a 27 Cancer 45 Midheaven, and I feel this reflects Lennon's emotional nature and creative talent clearly. It also places the Moon, ruler of the Midheaven, on the IC.

---

3. AMG.

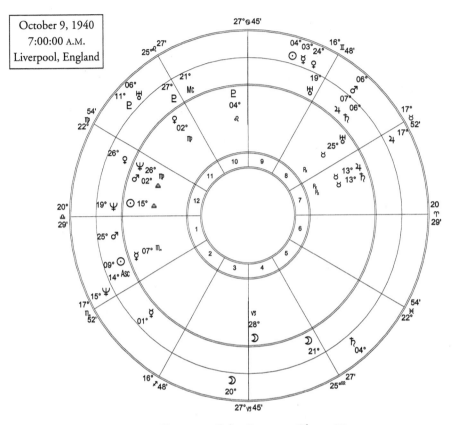

Chart 22. John Lennon Chart #1

During February of 1970, within a one-week time period, John Lennon wrote, recorded, and released a single called *Instant Karma*. This song rose to the top ten on the charts in both the UK and the U.S. The 7:00 P.M. chart for that time period has solar arc Neptune conjunct the Ascendant, solar arc Venus sextile the Midheaven, and solar arc Pluto semi-sextile the Midheaven.

A strong argument can also be made for the 6:30 P.M. time, as solar arc Neptune exactly opposes the Ascendant in this chart, and solar arc Jupiter is quincunx the Midheaven. The chart is included in this chapter on the Cancer Midheaven because Lennon's life exemplifies the nature of the third style of Cancer at the Midheaven. For him, the balance of water and fire energy resulted in periodic bursts of creative energy during which he produced his best work. Imbalance of these two energies also reflects the withering effect of excesses and consuming desire that marked most of the early 1970s for him.

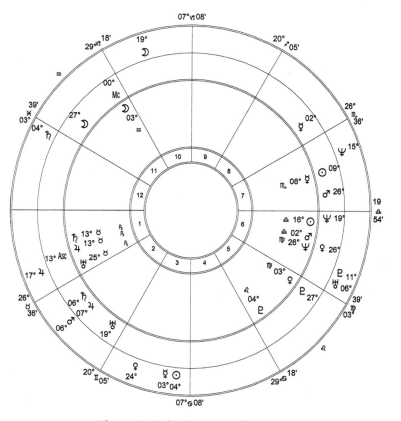

Chart 23. John Lennon Chart #2

Other Cancer Midheavens

David Bowie, January 8, 1947, 11:50 P.M., London, England

Charles E. O. Carter, January 31, 1887, 11:00 P.M., London, England

Stonewall Jackson, January 20, 1824, 11:59 P.M., Clarksburg, West Virginia

Frank Borman, March 14, 1928, 6:30 P.M., Gary, Indiana

Jean Harlow, March 3, 1911, 6:40 P.M., Kansas City, Missouri

Arthur Ashe, July 10, 1943, 1:55 P.M., Richmond, Virginia

Thomas A. Becket, December 21, 1118, 12:30 A.M., London, England

Geo. Armstrong Custer, December 5, 1839, 1:30 A.M., New Rumley, Ohio

Rainer Marie Rilke, December 3, 1875, 11:50 P.M., Prague, Czechoslovakia

Simon Wiesenthal, December 31, 1908, 11:30 P.M., Uuczacz, Ukraine

7

LEO
MIDHEAVEN

In the Northern Hemisphere the Leo Midheaven is usually less than 90-degrees from the Ascendant. This angle occurs Leo follows Cancer, the sign of the summer solstice. Generally this means that Leo Midheavens will tend to think for themselves and be less dependent on the world. If this angle is supported by many planets in the Eastern Hemisphere of the chart, the tendency will be emphasized, while planets in the west will tend to create a balance of introversion and extraversion. In the Southern Hemisphere this angle will be greater than 90 degrees and the reverse tendencies will apply.

Leo is a fixed fire sign. On the Midheaven it indicates an individual who consciously exerts his or her will. While Aries Midheavens are aware of their goals, Leo Midheavens are more aware of the path to the goal and the personal decisions along the way. No step is taken without conscious consideration of its effect on the outcome. When Leo Midheavens are self-aware, they make fine leaders. They know no fear and they demonstrate their authority clearly.

High Aspirations
Leo Midheavens set their goals high and have the staying power to achieve them. They know that persistence will gain them the goals they have set. Alchemically,

the fire of Leo is the sort used in the baking process. Pottery is merely clay before it is fired; afterward it becomes one of the most enduring of human artifacts. Leo Midheavens know this about themselves: they can endure through all sorts of trials and come out on top (they define "on top" as individuals, not as members of a group).

Ego-consciousness thrives in the fire of Leo. Leo Midheavens know they are better and stronger for the firing process. This knowledge can go two ways: first, Leo Midheavens often rise to whatever occasion life presents, appearing to be larger than life and more perfect. Courage and nobility rise like cream to the surface. On the other hand, Leo Midheavens can become arrogant to the extreme. Hitler presents the archetypal example of a man who has decided he is the best and his ideas are the only correct ones. He stubbornly held to his global plan in the face of imminent defeat, ignoring the advice of his generals. We all know little Hitlers; Charlie Chaplin gave us a humorous portrayal of such petty tyrants.

Desire to Achieve Social Status

Leo Midheavens seek the cream—they want to rise to the top socially. Jacqueline Kennedy provides an example of a woman who achieved the goal brilliantly. She is still held up as the model wife of a president. Grace Kelly is another individual who reached the top of her acting profession and then became the wife of a monarch, thus reaching the top twice. Both of these women avoided the pitfall of pretentiousness. They both shined so brightly that they are associated instead with social grace and were both tremendously popular in the U.S. and abroad.

Self-Confidence

Leo Midheavens know that they will be successful in their endeavors; they exemplify self-confidence at all times. This is because they have tempered their thoughts from childhood with the trials of growing up. They have tested themselves and found themselves worthy. This inner knowledge carries them farther than any outward success can do.

In the process of developing self-confidence and self-awareness, Leo Midheavens also acquire the ability to look good even when they are not feeling so powerful. It becomes a habit to present a confident face to the world. On the rare occasion when this is not possible, they become very private, revealing as little as possible.

Generosity

Leo Midheavens know two things about themselves: They are basically generous individuals; they lose nothing by being generous. Leo wants to share with the world; Leo Midheavens know that this desire is at the heart of their lives. Esoterically the Sun is the second ray of love/wisdom. Leo Midheavens realize that they demonstrate their love through generosity and that they develop wisdom in the process. True generosity means giving without any plan of a return—giving because they are able.

Leo Midheavens are probably not born generous; rather, they learn through experience when and where it is appropriate to give to others. Very difficult aspects between Midheaven and planets may indicate life experiences that have taught caution in this area. Then the Leo Midheaven must temper generosity with intelligent planning and decision-making.

Ability to Lead

Leo Midheavens know that they can be fine leaders. They have cultivated an awareness of others, and they have developed an inner sense of what is needed to motivate others skillfully. For Mohandas Gandhi, adherence to fundamental beliefs concerning nonviolence made him a consistent leader. Hitler, by contrast, used his knowledge of human behavior to control the people around him in destructive ways. Both were highly skilled, charismatic leaders.

Organizational Skill

Leo Midheavens know they have organizational capabilities of a highly developed nature. They can compete in the marketplace precisely because they can get an overview of vast projects and pay attention to the details. They grasp the grand strategy as well as the minute tactics involved in whatever game or activity they choose.

Freud is a good example of someone who knows how to play the game. As he accumulated data in his psychological practice, he began to see a pattern in his hysterical patients. He understood, as one patient after another revealed incestuous history from childhood, that the population was rife with child abuse. He also understood, as his colleagues and wife began to complain about his theory, that he would be destroyed professionally if he pursued it further. He therefore gave up this direction and changed the course of his research, emphasizing the Oedipal theory instead. His data could support more than one theory and he chose his direction because of expedience. He used his organizational skills to salvage his social position.

Hypersensitivity to Humor

Ebertin suggests this trait in the Leo Midheaven. Perhaps Ebertin knew that Leo Midheavens understand how exposed they are to public scrutiny. Humor is a way of telling people about their shortcomings; Leo Midheavens know a lot, but they may not be able to admit their own flaws. Thus, humorous jibes may be taken too seriously. Mary Schneider, a Denver-area astrologer, first put me onto the importance of the Midheaven where humor is concerned. She has a special grasp of the humor associated with each Midheaven, as well as the sensitivity associated with this point.

Of course, there is wisdom in humor concerning the Midheaven. We use humor to illustrate difficult concepts. We use humor to teach all sorts of things. Stand-up comedians invite us to examine social concepts. Shakespearean comedies reveal subtler truths about how we think and feel by placing characters in unlikely situations and letting the natural consequences develop. The Midheaven in our charts reveals how we understand humor and how we respond to it.

Resistance

Resistance exists in the time and space between what we have and what we want. Fixed signs on the Midheaven suggest individualistic stubbornness that reveals the quality of unconscious resistance. Leo Midheavens, usually generous and capable, can dig their feet in when they are overly attached to one certain path. Rather than change one's mind, the Leo Midheaven often withdraws from discussion altogether, refusing to continue to play at all if they don't like the rules.

When Leo Midheavens rejoin the game, we often are made to feel that they and they alone are responsible for the new rules. It seems as if they never left the playing field, or that they know so much that they stepped back to let the rule changes manifest—that they did this intentionally.

Perhaps the greatest gift Leo Midheavens give to others is that they encourage others to be individuals, and at the same time they hold the ground of the present. They encourage others to grow and change but never lose sight of the value of what has gone before. In this way they manifest the best of the unconscious Aquarian wisdom that bubbles up into consciousness. This is what Leo Midheavens know about leadership and about generosity. They often know when to bow out gracefully, or when to tenaciously hang on.

Capacity to Respond

All fixed sign Midheavens are capable of responding with sustained effort and are seen as being the ultimate in reliability. Look to the Leo Midheaven for qualities of warmth and courage, as well as dignity and authority. The Leo Midheavens know they can step in and command attention in difficult situations, causing desired changes to occur by force of personality. While the results are quick and definite, they may not endear Leo Midheavens to the object of their authority.

Leo Midheavens know the value of courage in situations where no other quality will suffice. They are able to impart this quality to others because they know it at the heart level of understanding. It is through love that Leo imparts courage to others.

No one can surpass the dignity of Leo; the Leo Midheaven knows the depth of character from which dignity proceeds. The edge which results is very interesting: Leo Midheavens can provide dignity to any situation through their presence. They can demand dignity from others in formal and informal situations. They can also strip dignity from friend and foe with one sentence, or one word. They know exactly what to do to make others feel either distinguished or inept. They may use this ability to control others; such control is not true leadership, but coercion. The true Leo leader never causes another person to feel humiliated, as they know the intimate pain involved. Leo Midheavens certainly would resort to such an undignified assault only as a last resort.

Sanity and Neurosis

The three thinking styles associated with Leo at the Midheaven include the following astrological correspondences:

1. The cusp of Cancer and Leo, or the movement from cardinal water to fixed fire.

2. The pure energy of the fixed fire sign itself.

3. The cusp of Leo and Virgo, or the movement from fixed fire to mutable earth.

These three relationships describe both the neurotic potential of Leo on the Midheaven and the sanity to be found there.

Cancer/Leo Cusp

The transition from a water sign to a fire sign exemplifies the dynamic of discriminating awareness in Buddhist psychology. The movement from cardinal water to fixed fire is the transition from the fluidity of water to fixed fire. Fixed fire sounds impossible, given the nature of the element. Neither Cancer nor Leo feels solid. By comparison, Sagittarius (a mutable sign) and Aries (a cardinal sign) are far better prepared to deal with the water to fire transition. There is a need for the Leo Midheaven to create and maintain a stable personality and environment in spite of constant change.

Because of the tension involved, Leo Midheavens are extremely easy to insult. They will take virtually everything personally. Instead of their characteristic depth of interpretation, they seem to be limited to one response—hurt feelings. At such times, the Leo Midheaven is without insulation, naked and defenseless. Imagine the surprise of their friends! Normally dignified conversationalists suddenly become silent and angry. You may not ever find out what set them off.

Inherent in the neurotic behavior is the sanity of this thinking style. The Leo Midheaven can generally interpret on several levels, always searching for the breadth of meaning in any remark. At such times they expand on a conversational tidbit, enlivening it with anecdotes and drawing information from others.

Where both Aries and Sagittarius are adept at change, Leo's strength lies in stability. To develop a sane approach to change, Leo Midheavens must understand the flow of all processes and accept the knowledge that their own psyches operate this way. Any perceived slowness is not a flaw or fault—it is a result of patterns developed over a lifetime. Leo knows that the proper temperature and length of time are needed to cook anything. Leo Midheavens have a unique sense of timing where psychic change is concerned.

The Pure Energy of Leo at the Midheaven

The second thinking style of the Leo Midheaven deals with the energy of the pure fixed fire sign. Resting in the energy of Leo reflects the pure energy of the fire element as it expresses through the fixed quality. The neurosis common to the pure Leo is the ability to avoid inconvenient facts about change. Ignorance—either not knowing or simply ignoring the facts—is particularly undignified when revealed in a Leo Midheaven. It manifests because of a fear of change, and the fear casts Leos in a poor light, showing them to be less than perfect. Sanity suggests allowing space in which change can occur, and even acting in a magnanimous way while doing so. Because the Leo Midheaven comes to understand the value and necessity of change, it becomes skilled in working with people, especially children, allowing them all the time they need to learn a new process. Inflexibly ignoring the facts grows into a strong, intuitive, steadying influence in the Leo Midheaven's life.

Leo/Virgo Cusp

The third thinking style of the Leo Midheaven is concerned with the transition from Leo to Virgo, or from fixed fire to mutable earth. Leo's greatest skill lies in stabilizing situations, so this neurosis will appear infrequently. Leo's fire is about using heat to cook, to harden pottery and steel, etc. Thus the Leo Midheaven looks good and exudes self-confidence when the focus is on the fire-earth interaction, where Aries resists becoming stable in Taurus and Sagittarius is in danger of dissipation. Leo's neurotic response might include doubt about whether the pot, now hardened, will really hold water. Will the food, now cooked, be palatable? Usually Leo is certain that all the proper steps have been taken and that things will turn out. Only when the Leo Midheaven is very off balance will this type of neurosis emerge.

Summary

The key to the sanity of the Leo Midheaven lies in the ability to create the space in which to move, to maintain that spaciousness in mind, and to encourage it in others. Leo consciously uses intuition as a practical tool. By cultivating spaciousness of mind, Leo is able to unify intuition and intellect and put them into action together.

Conscious Choice

The Leo Midheaven is the master of control of free will. The key phrase for this sign, "I will," demonstrates the strength of a lion. These people know that they are in control of their own destiny and that they can will situations to change to suit them, they can will events to move in specified ways. They teach the rest of us how to develop this essential human capacity just as our parents teach us everything we need to know as children.

The larger purpose of Mind is the unfolding of consciousness on physical, mental, emotional, and spiritual levels. Leo at the Midheaven is aware that this unfolding depends on the individual mind. According to Alice Bailey, Leo functions through sensitivity. Hypersensitivity is a pivotal problem for the Leo Midheaven. Leo Midheavens begin to have a positive effect on the world when they have been personally affected by the world, when they have become sensitive to their individual being, and when they respond to the soul as a conditioning factor as well.

Spiritual Growth

Enlightenment involves a healthy identification with creation. The energy of fire creates artifacts that outlast human life. Leo Midheavens create personal containers in which to process their own *prima materia*. They carry these containers forward into future lifetimes, containers made of will, developed by experiencing in the fire of ordinary physical existence. They are open to the facts that no material container is necessary, that we have physical bodies to have physical experience, and that we transcend physical requirements when we realize we are one with creation.

According to traditional Western astrology, the power of Uranus and Saturn are lessened in Leo, except for those at a sufficient level of initiation to respond to Uranus' energy. Saturn, then, is the only planet whose power is necessarily lessened in Leo. The very lord of karma holds less sway here. Leo Midheavens know the requirements of discipline but are not as limited as other signs by the power of Saturn. Leo may begin by stating, "I am an individual of significance," and end by stating, "I am that Unity in which everything exists."

Chaplin and Hitler—An Astrological Comparison

Charles Chaplin (chart 24) and Adolf Hitler (chart 25) were born within days of each other and share the Leo Midheaven. Setting aside all other astrological comparisons and focusing on the Midheaven, They show a remarkable difference in the way they chose to use will to control other people. Both had to work very hard to achieve success—neither was instantly on top.

Chaplin stated in his autobiography how he found his calling: "At the age of five I made my first appearance on the stage . . . Halfway through [my first song] a shower of money poured onto the stage. Immediately I stopped and announced that I would pick up the money first and sing afterward. This caused much laughter . . . I talked to the audience, danced, and did several imitations including one of Mother . . . In all innocence I imitated Mother's voice cracking and was surprised at the impact it had on the audience. There was laughter and cheers, then more money-throwing; and when Mother came on the stage to carry me off, her presence evoked tremendous applause. That night was my first appearance on the stage and Mother's last" (Chaplin, p. 21). This introduction to the limelight had a profound effect on five-year-old Charlie, who went on to a very successful career on stage and in film.

Hitler nearly achieved a comparable political success, but material from *Mein Kampf* indicate the vast difference in intention: "My adversaries . . . applied the one means that wins the easiest victory over reason: terror and force" (Bartlett, p.812). Here we see a diametric contradiction to Chaplin's view. Hitler used the same terror tactics that he claimed that his opponents employed, while Chaplin used laughter. Volumes have been written about Hitler's psychological state and how he arrived at this and other similar conclusions. His less conscious thinking function was warped in a destructive direction that was directed at the weak and ignorant. You need only rent an old Chaplin movie to know that he was doing quite the opposite. His films call upon the intelligence of the audience, and at no time do terror or violence become part of the audience response.

The *Great Dictator* was released in 1940 and brought Chaplain his first movie failure (solar arc Midheaven sextile Saturn indicates hindered growth). He was also having personal problems, including a paternity suit brought by Joan Barry and relationships with various women (solar arc Venus formed a semi-square to his natal Midheaven). Chaplin was able to learn from these events and grow from experience (transiting Neptune semi-sextile his Midheaven), and adjust his style via ego-conscious action (solar arc Midheaven quincunx his Mars). His career in movies continued until the mid-1960s.

Hitler was at the peak of his power in early 1940 when he engaged in the blitzkreig campaigns. By June the Axis powers controlled all of Western Europe from the Arctic, and Northern Africa as well. Like Chaplin, 1940 brought Hitler his first major obstacle in the Battle of Britain, and he was forced to rethink his invasion plans. Transiting Pluto conjuncted his Midheaven in October 1940 and made a retrograde station at 4 Leo 20 in November, with the last of five exact conjunctions occurring in June of 1942. During that year Hitler experienced

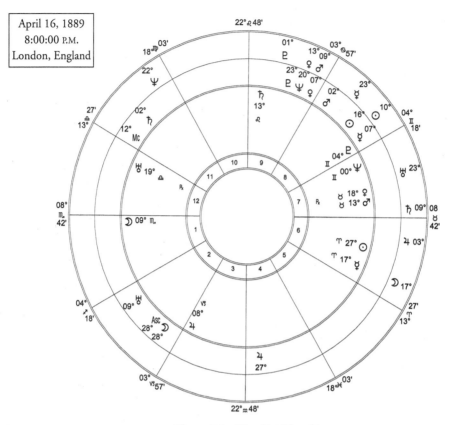

Chart 24. Charlie Chaplin

Rommel's defeat at El-Alamein in the Libyan Desert, the German Army's inability to take Stalingrad, and heavy bombing by the R.A.F. and U.S. Air Force. This conjunction of Pluto to his Midheaven signaled the changing of the tide of Hitler's military success.

Hitler did not have the benefit of a major aspect of his solar arc Midheaven to his chart in 1940. Such an aspect would have indicated the potential for ego-conscious action (as seen in Chaplin's Midheaven quincunx Mars). The solar arc Midheaven formed a sesqui-square to the Sun-Mars and Sun-Venus midpoints, reflecting the intense agitation at the time. Hitler showed his stubborn, one-sided drive for power (Sun-Mars), but little of the potential harmonious side of the Sun-Venus aspect. By the time the Midheaven moved up to quincunx his Mercury, Hitler was too far down the road of ruin to adjust to the advice and military intelligence of his officers.

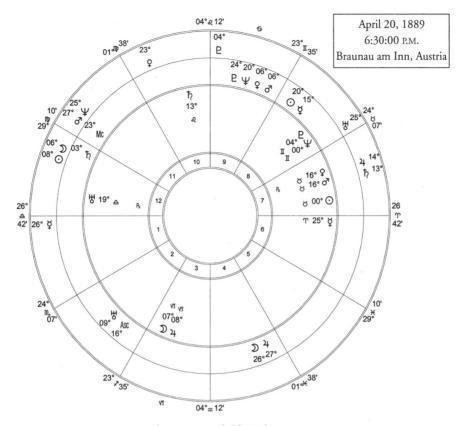

Chart 25. Adolf Hitler

Looking to the psychological condition of the Midheaven again, we find that where Chaplin took his failures in stride, learned from them, and went on to make *Limelight,* which won him an Oscar, Hitler became even more entrenched in his stubborn desire to rule the world. He refused to look at the war logically, and therefore lost everything. It was his inflexible intellect that was his downfall. Chaplin, however, remains the standard where comedy is concerned.

Chaplin and Hitler show how similar potentials can lead to vastly different results. Both were skilled manipulators, but Chaplin was far better able to manifest the sense of freedom and precision of the sign in his stage and film work. Hitler chose a path lacking in nobility and based on fear, using his intellect to support his dictatorial style. Chaplin was no saint. He brought happiness to millions, but caused great pain for a few close friends and family members. Hitler slaughtered millions of people in his push for power, and may not have brought happiness to anyone.

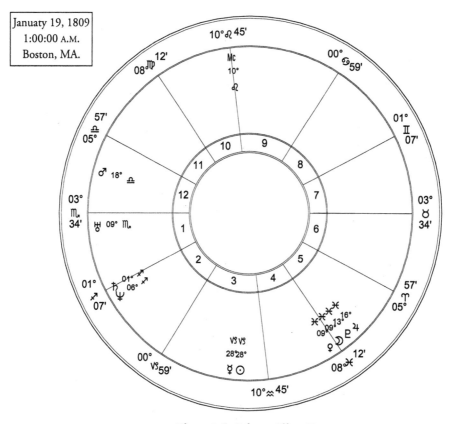

January 19, 1809
1:00:00 A.M.
Boston, MA.

Chart 26. Edgar Allan Poe

Edgar Allan Poe

Edgar Allan Poe exemplified the very best and worst of the Leo Midheaven (chart 26). "Poe has often seemed an embodiment of the satanic characters in his own fiction, the archetype of the neurotic genius. He left no diaries . . . and the vivid derangements portrayed in his writing and the tales of his own depravities (many of which he told himself for their shock effect) created a false portrait." (McMichael, p. 367). His reviews of other people's writing were merciless—he was called "the tomahawk man." Biographical material suggests that he may have been just as hard on himself.

The aspects to the Midheaven in his chart indicate the nature of his self-awareness. Quincunxes of the Midheaven to the Moon, Venus, and Pluto reflect the extremes of Poe's life. His own ability to evoke horror in his writing contrasts with the extremely corrosive style of his reviews of other writers. There is a powerful sexual drive present, as well as the capacity for artistic creation. At the same time, there is a capacity for licentiousness and the use of excessive force in expressing oneself. The crises in Poe's life are one measure of his ego-consciousness or lack thereof.

Jupiter forms a biquintile to the Midheaven, indicating the potential to achieve great success. While Poe was desperately poor during his life, his writings have continued to grow in popularity. His successful stories and poetry point to the fact that he had windows of clarity during which he was able to produce fine writing. The trine to Neptune addresses both his lack of self-awareness and his skill in taking romantic story lines and weaving them into great tales of horror. This trine is also one indication of Poe's mental disturbance.

What we know of Poe's life indicates that he was never able to achieve the balance and stability indicated by the Leo Midheaven. His creativity had the fire of Leo, but his personal life had no stable foundation. The loss of both parents early in life set him on a course of gambling, drinking, and general excess. Yet, he developed literary theories and mastery of form in his own writing that survive today, indicating his firm intuitive grasp of the medium.

Other Leo Midheavens

Clint Eastwood, May 31, 1930, 5:35 P.M., San Francisco, California

Mata Hari, August 7, 1876, 1:00 P.M., Leeuwarden, Netherlands

Werner Heisenberg, December 5, 1901, 4:45 A.M., Würzburg, Germany

Charlton Heston, October 4, 1923, 7:55 A.M., Evanston, Illinois

Pierre Salinger, June 14, 1925, 4:30 P.M., San Francisco, California

Janet Leigh, July 6, 1927, 2:15 P.M., Merced, California

Twyla Tharp, July 1, 1941, 2:24 P.M., Portland, Oregon

Aretha Franklin, March 25, 1942, 10:30 P.M., Memphis, Tennessee

Robin Williams, July 21, 1951, 1:34 P.M., Chicago, Illinois

Marcia Clark, August 31, 1953, 12:35 P.M., Oakland, California

Robert Oppenheimer, April 22, 1904, 7:00 P.M., New York, New York

Emily Dickinson, December 10, 1830, 5:00 A.M., Amherst, Massachusetts

Gregor Mendel, July 20, 1822 (rectified), 1:06 P.M., Troppau, Czechoslovakia

8

02° ♈ 16'

23° ♉ 34' ♄ ♃ ♂ ☉ 09° ♓ 15'

13° 05° 24° 25°

45' ♉ ♉ ♈ ♓ ♀

02° ☿

♓ ♓ 02°

50' 49' ♒ 18°

55'

VIRGO MIDHEAVEN

For births at northern latitudes, the angle between a Virgo Midheaven and the Ascendant is between 50 and 94 degrees, while southern-latitude births would result in angles wider than 90 degrees. The narrower angle for northern latitude births is an indicator that the Virgo Midheaven natives are somewhat more self-aware than signs like Aquarius which have much wider angles. Virgo Midheavens know how to analyze themselves and the world in detail. When this Midheaven is combined with many planets in the Eastern Hemisphere of the chart, one expects an individual who is a creator and mover in his or her life, acting on personal impulse rather than responding to others. If many planets fall in the Western Hemisphere, then self-awareness is balanced with a responsive attitude toward people and situations in one's world.

Critical Attitude

Virgo is a mutable earth sign. On the Midheaven it indicates a person who consciously serves by shielding, nurturing, and revealing Spirit. Virgo Midheavens are aware of the depth of their experience and the nature of the secrets to be found there concerning the powers of mediation to resolve paradoxical ideas and beliefs. The empathy of the Pisces IC drives the Virgo Midheaven to a life of service.

The Virgo Midheaven reflects a critical attitude. This capacity of mind ranges from supportive critique to petty or vindictive criticism. "It never hurts to look at your own experience and learn from it" is a balanced attitude of the Virgo Midheaven. A less balanced attitude might be expressed as "I don't see why *you* never examine your life." A positive critical attitude is evidenced in the careful research of scientists and the significant attention of certain psychotherapists to the details of their clients' inner lives. Such people have examined their own details, sorted them out to some degree and evaluated them in ways that can be delineated by aspects to the Midheaven from the planets.

Neatness

Virgo Midheavens know that they can tidy things up in the physical world as well. However, the developed Virgo Midheaven may find that while neatness does solve certain problems of organization, it is no longer a requirement for basic sanity. These people can live in relative chaos—they seem to be able to find what they need when they need it. Attitudes range from "Oh, I can find it if I ever really need to," to "I know precisely where everything is, so don't move anything." Typically there is rhythmic movement between creating chaos and creating order.

Advancement

The Virgo Midheaven knows that advancement in life does not require elaborate machinations, but will proceed just as well with direct simplicity. These people waste little effort on dissembling, but cut to the heart of situations. They are compassionate in such situations, yet they know the sheer power of the truth. In general, they are hard to trick because of the discernment which comes with careful analysis.

Virgo Midheavens can be skilled teachers because they know the process of learning details as part of the larger picture. As students, these people soak up all kinds of information and question anything that does not fit the larger picture. They often have longer attention spans because they have practiced deeper levels of observation. This is consistent with the fact that while Virgo is a mutable sign, it is also earth. While the outer appearance may be of slow change, the inner activity of the Virgo Midheaven may include multiple shifts of viewpoint.

Secure Livelihood

Virgo at the Midheaven likes the security of knowing what is going to happen from day to day and year to year. These people may hold the same career position for many years. At first blush, such desire for stability seems inconsistent with the mutable nature of Virgo; however, the earth sign's groundedness may want career stability in order that emotional and other personal issues will have a secure container in which to blossom and develop.

Ebertin mentions "striving for a secure livelihood and a permanent position in life" as aims of the Virgo Midheaven (Ebertin, p.68). Virgo Midheavens know that they can manage their lives, and they know they want the security of a steady income. The stress created by ups and downs does nothing for their health and well-being. Because they are economical, Virgo Midheavens require less money to live comfortably. The desire for a permanent position can work to Virgo's advantage. By remaining in the same position, there is the potential for advancement as well as the reality that they are comfortable with the people around them. They become a beacon that brings others back on track when life's difficulties arise.

Resistance

Resistance is the temporal transition between what exists and what you want to exist. What exists now is occupying space, so to speak, which can be made available for new thoughts. Resistance is the preservation mechanism which causes us to hold on to content which may no longer be serving any useful purpose. We hold on because we recognize the old stuff and feel secure in that knowledge.

Virgo Midheavens experience resistance through the capacity to analyze. They want to retain the knowledge gained through such analysis and may seek to retain all the data, not just the results. Such persons know they are pack rats, but little effort goes into sorting through the old junk to retrieve the few valuable items. Some of these people actually don't care about the junk; others don't wish to reveal their inner insecurities that are brought up whenever they are faced with giving or throwing away old things.

The crux of Virgo Midheavens' resistance is that they use analysis to create emotional insulation. As long as one remains in the analytical process, decisions do not have to be made and true movement does not need to occur. However, once this resistance is faced, the Virgo Midheaven can move forward with the sharply honed skills into new territory, transferring the inner analytical process to more public arenas.

Capacity to Respond

With Mercury as the ruler, Virgo at the Midheaven has the capacity to mediate in a variety of ways and is aware of this ability. Ego-consciousness relates so directly to the ability to mediate between inner and outer experience; thus Mercury-ruled Gemini and Virgo are strong at the Midheaven. Virgo skills of precise research and detailed study carry the individual toward self-understanding at the deepest levels. While not everyone needs to examine the details of inner spiritual life, the Virgo Midheaven will do so with a balance of economy and thoroughness.

It is the very act of self-investigation that allows Virgo Midheavens to act as mediators for others. They have had the personal courage and honesty to look at themselves and can be less unselfish guides for others, providing support by asking probing questions that reveal the inner workings of people's minds.

Sanity and Neurosis

The three thinking styles associated with Virgo at the Midheaven include the following astrological correspondences:

1. The cusp of Leo and Virgo, or the movement from fixed fire to mutable earth.

2. The pure energy of the mutable earth sign itself.

3. The cusp of Virgo and Libra, or the movement from mutable earth to cardinal air.

These three relationships describe both the neurotic potential of Virgo on the Midheaven and the sanity to be found there.

Leo/Virgo Cusp

The transition from a fire sign to an earth sign is the dynamic of expanded awareness in Buddhist psychology. The energy of fire changing to earth focuses on the fear of never having enough, or never being enough. This exaggerated emotional response leads to stinginess and indecision about how to simplify one's own life. The fear of not having is accompanied by smugness and self-satisfaction about what one does have. The fear of not being enough can manifestation as an inferiority complex: the fear itself creates an apparently opposite neurotic response.

The sanity that hides behind this neurosis has to do with unselfishness—that is, the knowledge that by creating space in one's environment, one invites something new to enter. Virgo Midheaven's generosity is not foolish, then. If nothing is ever given away, then no room exists for the new. The flow of the universe requires going as well as coming, and Virgo Midheavens judge this truth by examining the results of their own actions.

The Pure Energy of Virgo at the Midheaven

The second thinking style of the Virgo Midheaven deals with the energy of the pure mutable earth sign. Resting in the energy of Virgo reflects the pure energy of the earth element as it expresses through the mutable quality. The neurotic expression of pure Virgo energy manifests as worry and a fear of emptiness. This fear is partly responsible for whatever hoarding the Virgo Midheaven does—after all, it would be a bad thing to have an empty cupboard, empty room, and an empty heart. Then the individual worries about the very stuff that is occupying the space in order to provide comfort and security. Thus security issues become displaced in material possessions.

Here even more than in the above neurosis, knowledge of the reality and value of spaciousness is required. The sanity here is to discriminate among things, choosing those that one truly wants and needs, and letting the others go. There is strength in the internal sense of timing that tells the Virgo Midheaven when to let go. Establishing a rhythm of getting new things and disposing of old things is paralleled within the mind by the rhythm of admitting new ideas and purging old, out-worn patterns of thought and feeling.

Virgo/Libra Cusp

The third style of Virgo on the Midheaven is concerned with the transition from Virgo to Libra, or from mutable earth to cardinal air. The unique expression of neurotic energy here lies in the knowledge of potential inferiority. Hence the individual becomes critical of others in order to mask any self-doubt. In addition, Virgo focuses on those details that pertain to the immediate personal situation, ignoring other important information. There is much analysis and criticism of the motives of others. The naturally positive dexterity of Virgo becomes unhealthy manipulation.

Feelings of inferiority will yield to the accumulation of data concerning qualities that can only manifest if one is capable and dependable. The sanity of the earth-air cusp is to gain a perspective of objectivity, and then to apply that view to the practical matters at hand. One's own track record will belie feelings of inferiority. Because Virgo at the Midheaven generally indicates the ability to learn quickly and easily in career and public life, such a track record is almost inevitable. Knowledge of personal abilities is supported by facts.

Summary

To summarize the qualities of the Virgo Midheaven, each person has a unique analytical style that is reflected in aspects from planets to the Midheaven. At the base is the conviction that if one analyzes something enough, it will necessarily improve. We know that analysis alone cannot produce effective results; adherence to such a false premise can only lead to denial or dissatisfaction. When a sense of space develops, the Virgo Midheaven can use all its awareness to break through stagnation and move forward into uncertain territory. All the above expressions of sanity are accompanied by a strong sense of timing and are grounded in benevolent motivations.

Creativity

Virgo Midheavens know how to recognize creativity in themselves and in others. Mercury imparts verbal skills which can lead to literary creativity; there is often a strong scientific interest which leads to research (to be satisfying, it must have creative applications which can be predicted and guided). The highest expression of creative mind for the Virgo Midheaven is the wisdom called *Buddha Mind*. Buddha Mind develops when the mind is opened to broad possibilities and unhampered by limiting neuroses.

The Virgo Midheaven knows that simplicity is a virtue. This knowledge extends into every area of life. Simple food is good for one's health; simple clothing has elegance and style; examining the parts of a problem individually and then fitting them together into a pattern can solve difficult problems. This individual can also acknowledge the complexities of our inner spiritual and emotional lives. Perhaps the greatest strength lies in the ability to examine the parts without removing them from the whole, but by focusing on them in their natural setting.

Virgo Midheavens know their communication skills. They are transformed through communication directly. While they are capable of becoming skeptical and critical, they also employ language as a healing tool in their daily activities. When neurotic, the Virgo Midheaven knows that looking out for number one is essential. The sanity of Virgo is expressed through benevolent guidance of others into more spontaneous and creative pathways.

Conscious Choice

Virgo Midheavens exercise free will through analytical and communication skills. The ability to examine processes suggests a focused meditation style. By focusing the mind clearly, Virgo creates a spacious environment in which judgment and unselfishness can develop. Without the space free will is severely hampered. Thus the Virgo Midheaven cultivates health and honesty, and at the same time develops a tolerance for open, unfilled space. Then and only then the details of contemplative process can reveal themselves.

Spiritual Growth

Three principles become evident as the Virgo Midheaven seeks enlightenment:

1. There is an economy of mind that avoids stinginess of ideas and maintains a utilitarian approach. Skillful calming of the mind permits larger concepts to enter and to become comfortable.

2. There is a sense of universal time and one's movement within it. One understands the rhythm and current of events, perhaps even physically feeling the relative speed and quality of planetary and other energies.

3. One develops the capacity to tolerate uncertainty. Precision in action is focused on a compassionate awareness of others and their needs; it is no longer self-serving because the individual no longer needs exaggerated emotional defenses.

Meditation is important to the Virgo Midheaven. In order to reveal the inner light of consciousness, the Virgo must quiet the analytical conscious mind. In this way one discovers the true knowledge of the inner self and its relationship to the infinite. The profound knowledge of outer form the Virgo Midheaven in all material and social activities; the deeper awareness of the soul's activity provides spiritual and emotional security in the most difficult circumstances.

Esoteric astrology emphasizes the germinating energy of Virgo. The creative power of life becomes known to the Virgo Midheaven as an integral part of the self. As any feelings of separation from the creative force of Consciousness are removed, the Virgo Midheaven comes to know his or her role in the larger creative process of Universal Mind.

Timothy Leary

Timothy Leary placed himself at the heart of several controversies during his life, and had a profound influence in numerous venues (chart 27) (www.leary.com/Biography). He founded the League for Spiritual Discovery. Through this vehicle he advocated the legalization of LSD and marijuana by supporting their use in religious sacraments. He researched the use of hallucinogenic drugs in psychotherapy, but his work with prison inmates was curtailed when LSD was made illegal. His influence within the counterculture was related to the use of drugs. He refused to stop working with LSD after it became illegal, and he spent several years in prison because of his drug involvement.

He advocated the use of group therapy long before it was popular. His achievements went unrecognized by the APA for nearly fifty years. His public approach to his own death transition was a reflection of his radical approach to life. Because his ideas were so radical, he alienated the establishment, but became an icon for generations of young people, whom he encouraged to "turn on, tune in, drop out." By facing death in such a public way, he has made it possible for millions of people to look at this life transition in a new way.

Reading the facts about his life does not reveal the essence of Timothy Leary. The words feel flat compared to the texture of his ideas and the impact he had, especially on young people, from the 1960s onward. Timothy Leary believed that when you change yourself, you can then change everything around you. LSD and other drugs only serve as a way to jump-start the personal change process. Leary did not support the drugs-for-fun-and-profit mentality that arose in the '70s.

His interest in the computer revolution is directly related to his ideas about change. Computers, he felt, can be used to serve the purpose of evolution of group mind by providing a venue for dialogue across political and social boundaries.

The Virgo Midheaven reflects the attention to detail that Leary exemplified in his psychiatric research and his later interest in computer programming. The

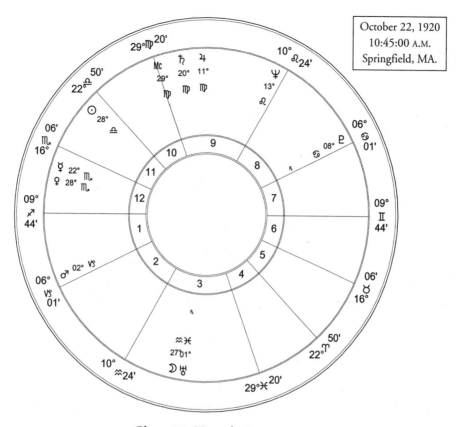

Chart 27. Timothy Leary

opposite sign of Pisces is indicative of the well of sympathetic and compassionate thought that drove his work and caused him to drop out of the traditional academic environment to pursue his research in the private sector.

Abraham Lincoln

Lincoln's mood changes were startling to the people around him (chart 28).[1] He could be outgoing and humorous, but then become withdrawn and sad. Of himself he said, "I have no other [ambition] as great as that of being truly esteemed of my fellow men, by rendering myself worthy of their esteem" (Oates, p.40). He was ambitious, yet utterly honest in his dealings.

---

1. Stephen B. Oates, *Abraham Lincoln: The Man Behind the Myth* (New York: Harper, 1984).

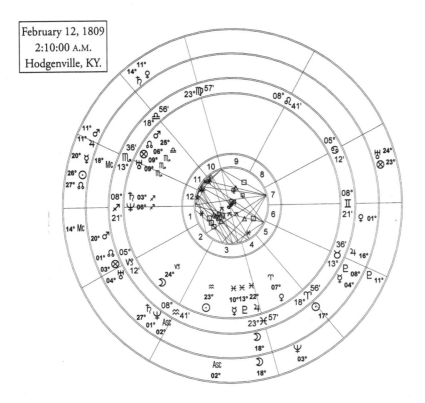

Chart 28. Abraham Lincoln

"One side of Lincoln was always supremely logical and analytical. He was fascinated by the clarity of mathematics and often spoke and wrote with relentless logic. . . . Yet this same Lincoln was superstitious, believed in signs and visions, contended that dreams were auguries of approaching triumph or doom" (Oates, p. 40). The first half of this quotation speaks to the power of the Virgo Midheaven in Lincoln's chart, while the second sentence is directed to the expression of the Pisces IC. Lincoln was very much aware that the mind was greater than the conscious mind. His own writings record dreams that he felt were significant.

At the time of the Gettysburg Address, November 19, 1863, Lincoln had solar arc Pluto sesquisquare the Midheaven. This is a strong indicator of his position as president, but also his position as leader of the Union Army. He had to gather his resources to concentrate on the war, while remembering his aims and not falling prey to disputes concerning his decisions.

Where does the inner strength come from—the strength to maintain one's moral position and to guide a nation through a civil war? Lincoln had the Moon trine the Midheaven in his birth chart. The Midheaven also opposed Jupiter, indicating his powerful desire to succeed in life. Transiting Uranus formed a trine to both the Sun and Mars in Lincoln's natal chart, and was just past a square to the Midheaven, indicating the heightened state of tension Lincoln must have felt at the time. In everything he did, and certainly in his preparation of this speech, Lincoln was focused on his goal of union and reform, yet he spoke to the dedication of those who had fought and died to achieve those objectives.

Sugar Ray Robinson

There is conflicting birth data for Sugar Ray Robinson (chart 29). Marc Penfield gives a birth date of May 3, 1921 (Robinson, p. 140), as does *AstroDatabank*, but other sources give a date of 1920. In the natal chart Robinson had Saturn conjunct the Midheaven. This placement clearly defines the limitations against which Robinson had to struggle to develop a career as a boxer. He had to stick to his objectives despite the racism and other barriers he faced. I imagine that the threat of ending his career if he refused to fight was an obstacle he could not see his way around. The Midheaven is quintile both the Ascendant and Pluto, reflecting his superior fighting ability. He used his strength to create a style. The Sun trine the Midheaven indicates a fortunate condition of practical surefootedness. The biquintile to Venus is indicative of the creative harmony that made Robinson great.

This powerful fighter also exemplified the heart of spirit when he begged his trainer not to make him fight a particular boxer. He had had a dream that in the fight he killed his opponent. He was told that he had to fight, and that if he refused, it would be the end of his career. Against his own better judgment, Robinson entered the ring on June 24, 1947. After several rounds, a powerful punch connected, the opponent fell to the mat, and died. We can only imagine how Robinson felt after this fight. Such an event, preceded by a vivid dream foretelling the outcome, must have rocked his world.

This fight occurred a full twenty years before Robinson won the middleweight title for the fifth time, when he was nearly thirty-eight years old. Robinson was a brilliant fighter, with a viciousness in his style as well as tremendous staying power. According to boxing aficionados, Robinson was an artist.

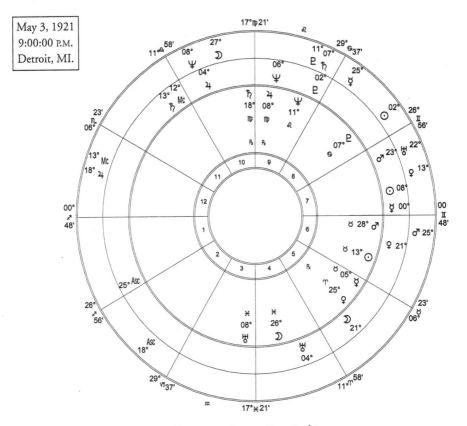

Chart 29. Sugar Ray Robinson

There is conflicting birth data. According to Marc Penfield, on the day of the fight transiting Neptune was in the minute of the station, turning to go direct. It formed a square to natal Pluto, quincunx to natal Uranus, and semi-sextile to natal Jupiter. Midheaven involvement in aspects included transiting Pluto sextile the solar arc Midheaven, indicative of the power of Robinson's mind at the time. The solar arc Midheaven was quincunx the natal Sun and sesqui-square Mars. Transiting Jupiter was sextile the Midheaven. As with many of the examples in this book, there are a multitude of other aspects, but the Midheaven involvement by itself clearly shows that Robinson was tuned into himself. He knew his own power and dreamed the outcome of the fight correctly.

Other Virgo Midheavens

Gary Gilmore, December 4, 1940, 6:30 A.M., McCamey, Texas

Martin Heidegger, September 26, 1889, 11:30 A.M., Messkirch, Germany

Gore Vidal, October 3, 1925, 10:00 A.M., West Point, New York

Shirley Temple Black, April 23, 1928, 9:00 P.M., Santa Monica, California

Elvis Presley, January 8, 1935, 4:35 A.M., Tupelo, Mississippi

Jack Nicklaus, January 21, 1940, 3:10 A.M., Columbus, Ohio

Maria Callas, December 3, 1923, 7:00 A.M., New York, New York

Friederich Nietzsche, October 15, 1844, 10:07 A.M., Lutzen, Germany

Isabel Hickey, August 19, 1903, 12:15 P.M., Boston, Massachusetts

9

LIBRA MIDHEAVEN

In the Northern Hemisphere Libra Midheavens are less than 90 degrees from the Ascendant. The farther the birth location is from the equator, the closer the angle between the Ascendant and Midheaven. In the northern United States, Canada, and Europe, the angle approaches 30 degrees, revealing that, for all their seeking of harmony in the environment, Libra Midheavens are actually rather self-motivated and less concerned with responding to others. This is, of course, subject to the placement of the planets. Many planets in the Western Hemisphere would counteract any self-willed qualities with affability and consideration.

Libra is a cardinal air sign. At the Midheaven it indicates a person who knows the depth of the thinking process. Meditation is a natural function for Libra Midheavens, who seek balance in everyday activities and use contemplative practice to approach that balance of mind. Meditation leads to deeper spiritual awareness and also provides a container for the knowledge that Libra gathers. Intellect and intuition meet here and form a synthesis of understanding for the ego-conscious Libra Midheaven.

Harmonious Demeanor

Libra Midheavens demonstrate harmonious behavior most of the time. They find no logical reason for being unpleasant. At the same time they often find no logical reason for being sincere. They know that they are acting a role for the benefit of others. Libra Midheavens are very capable of using the knowledge they have about people in general, and other individuals in particular, to smooth the social path for themselves. The individualized Libra is aware of this strategic behavior and can drop it when necessary, reverting to an honesty that is both surprising and refreshing.

Sponsorship from Others

Because Libra Midheavens are set on cooperation as a social requirement, they expect cooperation in return, in the form of support for their ideas. This kind of sponsorship comes to them when they are performing at a high skill level. People will not support an inept individual, regardless of the Midheaven they have. Libra Midheavens, however, attract greater support to themselves through their ability to inspire a sense of partnership with others.

According to Ebertin, advancement in career of the Libra Midheaven comes through sponsorship by other people (Ebertin, p. 69). Michelangelo had to have a sponsor in order to create art; Martin Van Buren could not elect himself; Jack Benny had television sponsors to pay for his program. Sometimes, then, it is easy to perceive how Libra Midheavens have relied on others for their career position. Even when it is not so clear, we can depend on the fact that the Libra Midheaven knows who has been supportive and who has not.

Cooperation or Exploitation

Libra Midheavens, when well integrated, have an inner knowledge of the range of partnership, from cooperation to exploitation. They work with others without expecting others to work for them. The atmosphere around such a leader is filled with challenges, but is also filled with an expectation of success and a certain inspiration. Libra expresses inner knowledge through words and actions that create an atmosphere of consideration. When a situation begins to fail, however, Libra Midheavens can become indecisive or impatient, expecting others to carry on by themselves. If one's associates have been selected carefully, they will be able to carry on without depending on Libra for direct support. In such a situation

Libra Midheavens have given something of their self-awareness to others, a true test of their ego-consciousness.

Material Interests

Libra Midheavens know they are concerned with the material side of life as well as the intellectual. The love of harmony and beauty inspires them to surround themselves with lovely things—they don't wish to be in unpleasant surroundings. For Libra the environment is part of the mechanism for achieving and maintaining balance. This can occur on any economic and social level; large amounts of money are not required for creating relative harmony and beauty. What is required is some conscious effort to create balance in the physical environment in order to inspire balance on the mental, emotional, and spiritual planes. Not as acquisitive as other signs, Libra Midheavens know when it is time to let go of the old.

Conscious of Social Position

Libra Midheavens know where they stand in terms of social position. They also are clear within themselves about where they wish to be. Thus one finds individuals who are on top and let others know; there are also individuals who don't care to climb at all, but find a comfortable position among their friends at whatever social level. More significant, I think, is Libra's ability to develop harmonious relationships with people at any social level. Libra Midheavens know that they can carry on a conversation with anyone. They also know that they can manage just about any situation through perceptive awareness. The more such events Libras have experienced, the more adept they become, until they are welcome guests at any gathering, regardless of their position.

Success Through Adaptation

Libra Midheavens adapt to conditions. Social position is only one condition in which this adaptation is an advantage. Libra, walking the path of balance between opposites, has brushed up against both sides of every issue, every decision. They know that a little movement in either direction will seem like agreement to others. Thus they are able to inspire trust in people without making a major shift in their own position. This quality is integral to Libra's success in the world. They know where the balance is, they adapt to the surrounding ambiance, and they act from the heart.

Libra Midheavens can fall into a pattern of being pleasant simply for effect. When they do this, they are not acting from the heart, but are insincere as a matter of convenience. Such a posture requires them to leave the middle path; it also creates mistrust in others who recognize the lack of sincerity. Whenever and wherever false pleasantness is found, one suspects the motive. Libra Midheavens know they can fall into such behavior; they also know how to avoid it. Finally, they know that they will sometimes be accused of insincerity when they are sincere. No one is uniformly accepted without question. The strong Libra Midheaven knows that this is a fact of life.

Resistance

Resistance occupies the time and space between what one has and what one wants. For Libra Midheavens, resistance focuses on the desire to maintain harmonious feelings when it is time to engage in battle. Balance and refinement are one end of a spectrum of possibility that includes outrageous behavior and extreme ideas. Libra Midheavens know that they are at a disadvantage in such situations, yet they are skilled in adaptation. When the wind changes, Libra can usually follow it, finding new tactics for the hopefully temporary imbalance. Only when the necessary action seems too harsh will Libra resistance emerge.

There is a certain risk of impressionability. They can be somewhat blind to the realities of a situation, sympathetic to those who push for change, indecisive about their own choices. If Libra Midheavens have developed ego-consciousness, they will be aware of their point of equilibrium and will be able to reach that balance through contemplative practice or even by simply thinking about balance. They know about duality and recognize the polarity in everything. Thus they realize that there is no letting go; rather there is a movement along a continuum which becomes possible. Following someone's lead is not all that dangerous; one can retreat or take an entirely new direction as needed.

Capacity to Respond

As the point of equilibrium of the equinox, Libra Midheavens know that they can reach out to others without losing their own position. Thus they can respond easily and freely to a variety of situations. They can draw upon information from many sources in order to help solve a problem and the integrated Libra mind is able to synthesize solutions quickly and easily. There is integration between intellect and intuition, a balance between individual desire and love of a spiritual nature. Understanding this balance, Libra Midheavens can reach outside themselves to help others and retain equanimity as well.

Sanity and Neurosis

The three thinking styles associated with Libra at the Midheaven include the following astrological correspondences:

1. The cusp of Virgo and Libra, or the movement from mutable earth to cardinal air.

2. The pure energy of the cardinal air sign itself.

3. The cusp of Libra and Scorpio, or the movement from cardinal air to fixed water.

These three relationships describe both the neurotic potential of Libra on the Midheaven and the sanity to be found there.

Virgo/Libra Cusp

The transition from an earth sign to an air sign embodies the dynamic of effective action. The movement from mutable earth to cardinal air is the transition from meticulous attention to physical details to a refined and broadened perspective. The transition from Virgo to Libra brings the individual to a crisis point. The seeming security of acute attention to every detail is replaced by the hawk's-eye view of the larger picture. There may be an intense desire to get one's feet back on the ground—sort of an acrophobic reaction to the broader perspective. They may try to focus on the details in order to avoid the big picture and their fear of it. There may also be a withdrawal from social contact that is supposed to reduce the fear, but which serves only to isolate them from the very situations that provide balance.

Sensitivity to Libra Midheavens' point of balance can be an destabilizing experience. Yet the power of this Midheaven lies in the ability to move between the energies while preserving one's balance. Libra Midheavens know the middle path is narrow and straight; they see others wandering around, from one side of issues to the other, more or less unconsciously. The Libra who has risen above the petty transitory details of events and situations can see the long-term results of present actions. It is like driving a car: if you look at the end of the hood you cannot see where you are going. If you look down the road you can keep the car in the center of your lane more easily. For Libra Midheavens, the details of each hour or day are not as important as their life path.

The Pure Energy of Libra

The second thinking style of Libra involves the energy of the pure cardinal air sign. Resting in the energy of Libra reflects the pure energy of the air element as it expresses through the cardinal quality. The challenge is to stay with the spaciousness of the air element. Libra Midheavens are masters at existing in the space between opposites, so the neurosis is not the fear of too much space. Rather, it is the fear of becoming too solidly grounded in the physical realm. At the same time, there is anxiety over allowing desires to get out of control. The loneliness of remaining in balance is intense. Isolation becomes painful. Yet the fear of slipping prevents effective movement.

If that pain can be superseded by the larger awareness of compassion, Libra Midheavens become masters of their own feelings. They cease to be caught on the wheel of karma, but function through informed activity. From within the narrow path between opposites, Libra Midheavens know that they can and will make skillful choices.

Libra/Scorpio Cusp

The third thinking style of the Libra Midheaven is concerned with the transition from Libra to Scorpio, or from cardinal air to fixed water. Because we normally associate motion with both water and air, this cusp has built-in difficulties. Fixed water is ice—cold and resistant to change. The arrogance of Libra Midheavens is that they have the best perspective, that they know everything. The fact is that they are restricted to a life on the edge between too much thought process on the one hand and frigid, rigid feeling on the other. They sometimes find that they are unable to experience much at all. They have desires because they are physical beings. They also have an intense well of angry energy at their disposal. They can be boiling mad or they can exhibit icy hatred. The sanity of this cusp lies is in discovering the calm clarity of still water—the clarity to be found when intellect and feeling align with one another. Then water is fixed—not by being frozen, but by being utterly calm and clear.

Creativity

Creativity for Libra Midheavens lies in making works of true beauty. This can occur in any area of life and can encompass physical objects, ideas, feelings, and spiritual beauty. Physical art works are the most obvious form of harmony and beauty. Libra Midheavens know how to infuse their work with a timelessness that inspires others. Music and poetry have the same potential, if not the physical form. Man alone among the animals of earth has learned to preserve something of himself through the use of language, either verbal or musical, and conveys cultural meaning to future generations through these physical media.

The reason Libra Midheavens can produce these and other works of art lies in their attention to the balance between opposites. They are aware of opposition of artistic element, of counterpoint in music, of the possibilities of language to convey subtle thoughts and feelings. They also are aware enough to recognize the path that is right for them, close to the center but revealing something about the polarities that surround them.

Conscious Choice

Libra Midheavens know that they often acquiesce to others for the sake of convenience. They also know that this accommodation is never threatening to their individuality. They can be sympathetic without being indulgent; they can be considerate without becoming unctuous; they can demonstrate true compassion without falling into a pattern of doing whatever other people say they should. It is like a high-wire act: you can carry someone with you, but must remember the requirements of the wire at all times. You cannot allow the other person to pull you off balance or you will both fall.

Other people become irritated with Libras because they seem to be aloof and sometimes unavailable, and Libra Midheavens know that they seem this way at times. They also cultivate appreciation of others and can be rather romantic about it. They are generous in their opinions of others and may even need to create tests in order to convince themselves of shortcomings. This comes not from a sense of deep loyalty but from an idealistic belief that everyone is always doing his or her best. They are exacting in their expectations and can be deeply disappointed when others let them down. They expect the best in terms of cooperation; they give the best in terms of inspiration. They are able to do this because they understand that free will guides everyone's choices.

Spiritual Growth

If Libra Midheavens were so unimaginative that they never became aware of the polarities on either side of them, they would never achieve enlightenment. They need to tip one way or the other from time to time to understand the precariousness of the path. They need to experience what happens if they make a choice. They need to know that the center path is not for everyone. Only through this self-awareness can they experience or project true compassion. When Libra Midheavens have detoured and come back to the path, they have developed self-awareness. When they produce marvelous works of art and discover that other people find meaning in them, they become enlightened. When they are able to surround themselves with harmony and order on every level, and when they are able to share these things with others, then they have become realized.

Coco Chanel

Coco Chanel was a woman designing for women (chart 30). As such she tailored clothing to suit the demands of feminine life, instead of catering to a "look" that hobbled or corseted women, thereby limiting their ability to move freely. Coco Chanel said, "A dress made right should allow one to walk, to dance, even to ride horseback" (Rodden, p. 155). This statement certainly addresses the Libra Midheaven sense of harmony of form.

Mars, the ruler of the IC, forms a trine to the Midheaven. This is indicative of the energetic flair of Chanel's work. She drew on her basic sense of freedom and action to provide what women wanted and needed. The Chanel suit's enduring appeal is evidence that she partnered effectively with women in designing their clothes. The Mars aspect is indicative of Chanel's comfortable relationship with herself—her ego-conscious action in pursuit of her career goals.

She also has Sun sextile the Midheaven. She was able to express her goals well enough to convince an investor when she started out with a hat shop, and to grasp the opportunities that came her way. She knew her mission was to successfully provide great looking, serviceable dresses for women around the world.

Chanel, at the age of seventy, revived her business with the designs of the '20s that women loved so much. At that time the solar arc Midheaven was quincunx Saturn in the sixth house, a strong indication of the urge to re-enter the design

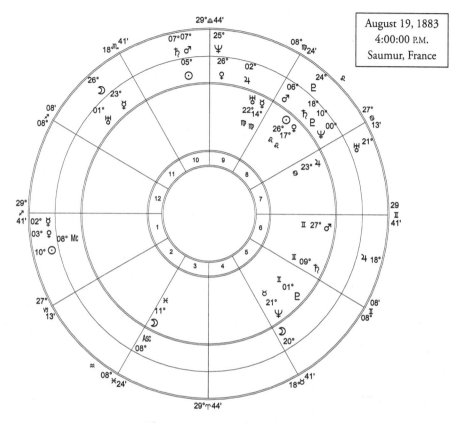

Chart 30. Coco Chanel

world. Solar arc Neptune was past the square to the Midheaven; transiting Neptune conjuncted Venus, ruler of the Midheaven, in January and again in November of 1954 (the first contact was in 1953). Solar arc Venus sextiled the natal Sun and trined Mars (ruler of the IC). This reflects the condition of being able to draw on resources deep within herself as well as the opportunity to gain prominence once again as a designer. Solar arc Saturn is past the conjunction to Venus in the eighth house, suggesting earlier changes in her personal life (perhaps financial) that led to her decision to begin again as a designer.

The Chanel look has survived to the end of the millennium as a basic element of the career woman's wardrobe. A woman who designed clothing with real women in mind, long before feminism was popular, Chanel proved that with the right approach, a woman could succeed on her own merits.

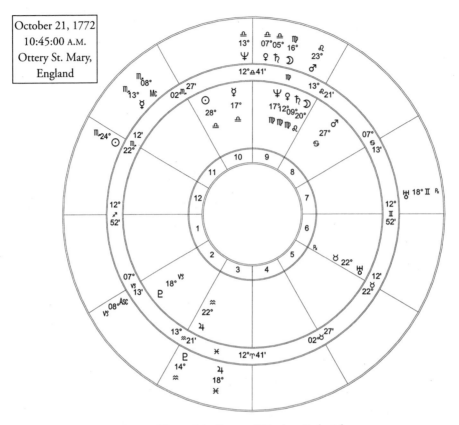

Chart 31. Samuel Taylor Coleridge

Samuel Taylor Coleridge

Coleridge fell from the center path of balance into severe drug addiction when he was about thirty-five years old (chart 31).[1] He had been using laudanum to treat episodes of pain, and ultimately was totally dependent on opium, though he understood that the drug was worse than the ailment. Even so, he was able to produce a number of works on literary and philosophical topics. Many of his poems were written in a single sitting. It seems that his genius arose in brilliant moments that were somewhat disconnected from each other.

Coleridge's writing is the foundation of modern fantasy. The simple definition of fantasy—writing about events that are impossible, or highly unlikely, does not consider the integration of elements of myth and legend into storytelling.

---

1. M. H. Abrams, ed., *Norton Anthology of English Literature*, vol. 2, rev. (New York: W. W. Norton, 1968), p. 211.

Coleridge felt that fantasy is only an echo of higher imagination. He earned his reputation as a poet with a few works, and held his reputation as one of the great minds of his age with his critical works.

Coleridge's birth time is between 10:45 and 11:00 A.M. With both of these two times, the Midheaven falls in the second decanate of Libra, and both provide convincing rectification data. Using the earlier time, we find that his solar arc Midheaven sextiled Saturn and solar arc Ascendant had entered the second house at the time he published "Rime of the Ancient Mariner," considered by many to be one of his best works. This poem is a fine example of the dark mystery that forms the heart of English Romanticism, The distinction between "high" and "low" fantasy in modern literature stems from Coleridge's ideas directly.

Because of the 50 degree latitude of birth, the fifteen-minute time difference results in a substantially greater change in the ninth-house cusp (I have used the Koch house system). Coleridge has the Leo Moon and Virgo Saturn in the ninth house when the earlier time is used, whereas these two are in the eighth with Mars using the later time.

The Libra Midheaven in the earlier chart sextiles the Moon. Here is the first indication of the source of his imagination: opportunities arose repeatedly, with each progressed and transiting aspect to Moon and Midheaven, to draw upon his inner voice. If the alternate time is taken, the Mercury conjunction and Mars quintile offer indications of the on-again-off-again burst of clarity that survive in his writing.

Cathy Rigby

Libra balance is of the essence of Cathy Rigby's life in two very different arenas (chart 32). At the age of only fifteen years, she rocketed into the public eye with her medal-winning competition at the Mexico City Olympics in 1968. In 1996 Cathy produced her video, *Cathy Rigby on Eating Disorders*, revealing her personal interest in a very different sort of balance—the emotional, psychological, and nutritional dynamics of self-image.

Cathy Rigby exemplifies the connection between earth and air—a predominant factor for early degrees of air signs at the Midheaven. Gymnastics is all about relating to the ground while seeming to fly. Her subsequent career demonstrates that her talents are not limited to one field, as she is an accomplished

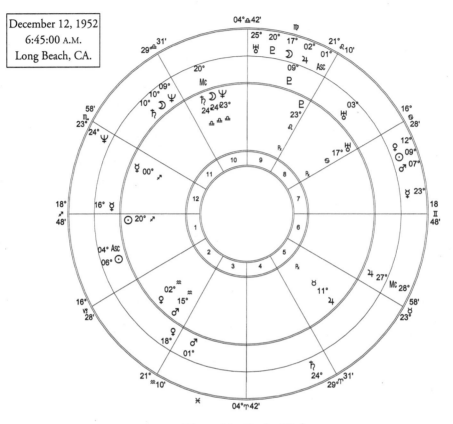

Chart 32. Cathy Rigby

musical performer and an actress. In addition, she has contributed to the understanding of eating disorders, helping to restore balance to the lives on many
young people.

During 1968, the year she won the first U.S. gymnastics medal for women at
the Olympics, Cathy had solar arc Midheaven sextile to her Sun and solar arc
Venus sextile to her Ascendant. Only fifteen years old, she experienced a defining
moment in her life by bringing focused self-awareness to her work, and by lifting
the beauty and balance of the sport to a new high for American girls.

Other Libra Midheavens

Vincent Price, March 27, 1911, 12:40 A.M., Saint Louis, Missouri

Robert Bly, December 23, 1926, 7:20 A.M., Madison, Minnesota

Raquel Welch, August 5, 1940, 2:04 P.M., Chicago, Illinois

Jodie Foster, November 19, 1962, 8:14 A.M., Los Angeles, California

B. F. Skinner, March 20, 1904, 2:00 A.M., Susquehanna, Pennsylvania

Hermann Hesse, July 2, 1877, 6:30 P.M., Calw, Germany

Eleanor Roosevelt, October 11, 1884, 11:00 A.M., New York, New York

Fred Astaire, May 10, 1899, 9:16 P.M., Omaha, Nebraska

Boris Becker, November 22, 1967, 8:45 A.M., Leiman, Germany

10

SCORPIO MIDHEAVEN

I n the Northern Hemisphere a Scorpio Midheaven is close to the Ascendant, sometimes less than 60 degrees apart. Birthplaces closer to the equator will have an angle of around 80 degrees. This means that Scorpio Midheavens are self-directed individuals, sure of what they want and how they should get it. If planets fall in the eastern half of the chart, this tendency will be magnified, while many planets in the west will balance the assertive style.

Scorpio is a fixed water sign. The sign is made up of striking paradoxes. Ice is fixed water, yet the traditional ruler of this sign is Mars, a fiery planet. The modern ruler, Pluto, is far from the Sun and surely cold, yet it is closely associated with Mars, and named for the god of the underworld, a traditionally hot place. Scorpio water may be better viewed as stagnant, like brackish water in marshes and swamps. It is in the depths of the swamp that we find the root of the beautiful water lily, and it is in the depths of the Scorpio Midheaven's consciousness that we find the essence of rebirth and self-realization.

While the opposite sign of Taurus reflects the ability to understand the world of form, Scorpio Midheavens are equipped to understand the world of feeling. Forceful to the point of aggression, Scorpio Midheavens know that their intensity often overwhelms others. Their passion can express as regenerative healing or degenerate promiscuity. Unlike the Libra Midheaven, Scorpio enacts strong polarities, and the middle ground may be difficult to find.

Ambition and Ruthlessness

Scorpio Midheavens know the value of ambition. Their ambition is not the direct uphill drive of Capricorn. Instead, it involves the growing sense of personal power of Pluto, the ruler of Scorpio. These individuals develop personal will that they can strengthen only through experience. For some of them, even failures are positive steps in the organization and function of will.

Some Scorpio Midheavens believe they know more than they do. This leads to a ruthless exercise of power that creates certain types of gain, but only through the loss of something else. Ruthlessness reveals self-interest that belies true understanding. Scorpio Midheavens may invoke harsh measures—they know that this is occasionally necessary. Acting without regard for others, however, betrays a lack of self-awareness or capacity to moderate personal will with spiritual will.

Perseverance

Scorpio contains the possibility for emotions as cold as ice. Such a person can keep going to the very edge of doom to accomplish the task occupying center ground. Beneath the seemingly emotionless inevitability of personal drive, there lies a larger knowledge that the impossible can be accomplished with enough effort. Perhaps because Scorpio Midheavens have a somewhat different understanding of death as a transition, they are able to continue as though they are fearless.

The edge of doom is a precarious line. Scorpio Midheavens also know that they can push themselves too hard and too far. When the well of emotional strength dries up, Scorpio is left depleted and momentarily powerless. They need a safe place in which to revive themselves. I do not use the term "heal" because the Scorpio's problem lies more in becoming re-inspired than in becoming healed. For them, healing is self-willed and can occur very quickly. It is the drawing of the first breath of creative energy that sometimes seems so difficult. The trained mind alone allows this breath to occur.

Sympathetic Understanding

Scorpio Midheavens know that they understand some of the basic truths of human existence. This understanding allows them to be genuinely sympathetic towards others. True sympathy demands awareness (though not personal experience) of the plight of the other. Even in the moment of ruthless action the self-aware Scorpio Midheaven understands the effect on others. Scorpio Midheavens can also identify the resources that others bring to situations and can inspire others to use that potential.

Death and Transformation

Scorpio Midheavens understand the nature of death and birth and other transformations differently than other people. Because everyone has Scorpio in their chart somewhere, and many people have planets in Scorpio, everyone experiences transformations during their lives. Scorpio at the Midheaven lends a particular intensity to transitions. Death, one of the most profound transitions we must face, carries us into the unknown. It is a model for all other transformations. Any profound change—in fact, any change—involves the death of an old way of thinking and the birth of a new way.

When faced with major transformations, Scorpio Midheavens know that they can survive the changes. They know they will be changed, even transfigured. They know they will continue after the changes have occurred. Thus they know a great deal about helping others. The examples in this chapter address the sense of life mission, attesting to the power of focused will for Scorpio Midheaven.

Sense of Acquisition

The key phrase for Scorpio, "I desire," is a basic source of self-awareness for the Scorpio Midheaven. These individuals know the immediacy of desire. Sustaining the physical body demands a certain desire for food, water, clothing, and shelter at the very least. Intellect then develops other desires, and emotional capacities reveal still others. Even the spiritual nature of man ultimately reveals itself through desire.

Scorpio Midheavens know of their desires. The question becomes one of direction and emphasis. There can be intense jealousies and suspicions that accompany certain kinds of desire. By the same token, there can be creative, healing processes involved with intense devotion. There can even be self-sacrifice when the object of devotion is in need. The full range of potential exists and Scorpio Midheavens become aware of these possibilities as they face life. Scorpio at the Midheaven reflects the range available—it is individual ego-consciousness that determines the direction of desire.

Overestimation of Self

The power of the Scorpio Midheaven to reveal inner truths may develop into belief that is an endless source of energy. In such cases, the individual drives himself or herself so hard that the only possible result is physical exhaustion, and therefore emotional or even spiritual exhaustion. While it may take a great deal longer for the Scorpios to reach this point, it is an eventual result if they continue to push. Thus Scorpio Midheavens must learn the personal limits of physical and emotional energy, and not rely on a boundless spiritual bank account for protection.

This understanding of personal limits can translate into a powerful understanding of other people who are struggling. Scorpio at the Midheaven can distill a sense of boundaries or limits that can then be applied in interpersonal situations. Scorpio Midheavens are conscious of their individual style in decision-making and are also aware of which decisions are most difficult for them. They can help others to become aware of their own strength and how to use it. They can help others who must make difficult decisions, not because they know the particular situation, but because they know about hard choices.

Resistance

Resistance is the space between what exists and what we wish to exist. Scorpio, the sign of desire, meets resistance on a moment-to-moment basis. An unconscious Scorpio Midheaven only knows about raw desire. More conscious Scorpio Midheavens know something about the results of attaining what is desired. Thus, the more conscious Scorpio Midheavens become, the greater resistance they may encounter. Because what occupies one's conscious space now has been obtained through greater and greater effort, the attachments become stronger and stronger. It is even harder to move the old out of the way for the new.

By the same token, Scorpio Midheavens can be of powerful assistance to others. They have developed the courage to let go of people, things, and situations that have tremendous importance. This courage can be shared with others. When I am faced with the most difficult situations, I want the power of Scorpio behind me, supporting me. I can borrow some of that courage. The self-awareness of Scorpio at the Midheaven allows the transfer of courage in a very direct way. They can find the Scorpio in others and work with it directly. Obviously, astrologers can do this, too, as they can identify the role of Scorpio energy for their clients. Scorpio Midheavens often can do this intuitively.

Capacity to Respond

Because of the understanding of transitions and change, as well as the strength and personal courage they recognize in themselves, conscious Scorpio Midheavens are able to respond to difficult situations with skill and inspiration. Because they also know about the cruel, more discordant sides of themselves, they can draw on a complete range of possibilities.

Recently, I saw a story about a man who was trapped under a huge boulder. He had the courage, as well as the cruel knowledge, to amputate his own leg and crawl to find help. He captures the essence of the Scorpio Midheaven—we make decisions based on what we know about ourselves. He decided the only way out of that situation was to take action, so he did.

Sanity and Neurosis

The three thinking styles associated with Scorpio at the Midheaven include the following astrological correspondences:

1. The cusp of Libra and Scorpio, or the movement from cardinal air to fixed water.

2. The pure energy of the fixed water sign itself.

3. The cusp of Scorpio and Sagittarius, or the movement from fixed water to mutable fire.

These three relationships describe both the neurotic potential of Scorpio on the Midheaven and the sanity to be found there.

Libra/Scorpio Cusp

The movement from an air sign to a water sign is the dynamic of changing from air to water. In the swamp the rising mist can obscure landmarks and cause disorientation. This neurosis involves jumping to conclusions, taking objective information and surrounding it with emotional input that may or may not be appropriate. The extension of this process is to become angry and even aggressive, attempting to resolve difficulties through the application of force. The mental error lies in believing that one knows more than is there to know. Thus instead of perceiving the clarity of still water, we see the morass of emotional activity.

The sanity that accompanies this neurosis lies in the perception of clarity. We know that we can take factual input available and work with it, unencumbered by supposition. We can see reality for what it is. This sanity emerges from both the air sign of Libra and the water sign Scorpio. The astrological terms for air and water signs can both used to describe the sanity of Scorpio because the sanity is made up of intellect as well as feeling. It is in this combination that human beings reach their mental potential.

The Pure Energy of Scorpio at the Midheaven

The second thinking style of Scorpio at the Midheaven involves the energy of the pure fixed water sign. Resting in the energy of Scorpio reflects the pure energy of the water element as it expresses through the fixed quality. Scorpio Midheavens experience when they must remain in overly emotional situations. Conditioned by life to avoid excessive energy drain caused by emotions, the Scorpio Midheaven learns instead to seek the calm, intellectual high ground. To the extent that one does not understand the emotional continuity of life, Scorpio penetrates too deeply, provoking jealousy and other undesirable feelings, leading to excess.

The corresponding sanity lies in the self-awareness that allows us to experience deep emotions. Scorpio Midheavens come to know themselves as emotionally powerful beings. They learn to go deeply into their feelings as a matter of practice, not as an emergency option. They overcome the fear of the depths because they know that they will survive one way or another. They develop space in which to experience emotional periods.

Scorpio/Sagittarius Cusp

The third thinking style of the Scorpio Midheaven is concerned with the transition from Scorpio to Sagittarius, or from fixed water to mutable fire. There is an intense desire to experience everything, and to do it all at once. This compulsive behavior can lead to breakdown because there has not been time for adequate rest. There is an urgency in the emotional drives that emphasizes the destructive energy of Scorpio, causing degeneration of the physical body, distortion of mental and emotional understanding, and reduction of spiritual reserves.

Sanity lies in the capacity to achieve intimacy with the world and everything in it, while retaining a well of reserve. This is not aloofness or a reluctance to participate in the world. It is a refined ability to be responsive without losing one's center. There is a very conscious movement from the overt desire of Scorpio to the more spiritual aspiration of Sagittarius. These individuals earn the trust of others through their personal devotion to creative healing processes.

Summary
Part of the nature of water is to seek the lowest point. Scorpio Midheavens know that they can plumb the depths of both constructive and destructive emotions. They also learn that they can rise above those extremes, like the phoenix rising from the ashes of the past. They make use of the fertile resources of feeling, both positive and negative, to expand their self-awareness.

Creativity
Scorpio Midheavens find their creativity in the deepest emotional recesses. They know that they can make things happen. For example, they know that they can heal physical illness, using the power of the mind. Most of all they know how to facilitate change on many levels. For Scorpio, creative energy comes from understanding the dynamic relationship between life and death. Transitions hold the potential for positive change for Scorpio Midheavens. They are willing to approach the edge of doom and look over, seeing the inspiration for the next life, the next creative process in the smoke. Like the phoenix, Scorpio Midheavens know they will survive in the midst of change.

Conscious Choice
Pluto is a planet of will and power. Scorpio is infused with this energy and it colors the mental life of Scorpio Midheavens. Self-awareness for them means the unique understanding of the secrets of life and death processes. Free will rests in the knowledge that one's innermost being never dies. Other people know this intellectually. Scorpio Midheavens often know this through personal experience. They demonstrate the power of will through their courage in the face of trouble, through their healing presence in the face of pain, through their determination in the face of impossible obstacles. They know that the power of will lies not in overcoming obstacles, not in the ability to heal others, not in the resolution of problems, but in the courage, determination, and willingness to heal.

Spiritual Growth
When Scorpio Midheavens realize the true significance of death as a process for change, they become more self-aware. When they realize the healing power they

can share with others, they are spiritually healed. When they realize the value of devotion and determination in achieving their focused desires, they are enlightened. Scorpios in general, and Scorpio Midheavens in particular, have to muck around in the discordant, coercive, cruel, and distrustful parts of the mind in order to understand the equilibrium of their own consciousness as a whole. They understand Unity and grasp the joy of diversity within that Unity.

Carl Jung

Jung recognized that his own capacity to transmute the suffering of others, a noble expression of the Scorpio Midheaven, was limited to the scope of his ability to understand his own inner processes (chart 33). "All consciousness separates; but in dreams we put on the likeness of that more universally truer, more eternal man dwelling in the darkness of primordial night. There he is still the whole, and the whole is in him, indistinguishable from nature and bare of all ego. It is from these all-uniting depths that the dream arises" (Van der Post, p. 214). This statement captures the essence of Jungian psychology. It is in the dream that we can see the more primitive yet more natural image of ourselves, without the enhancements and editing of the ego.

According to Jung's biographer, Jung "had been born with an inferior 'sensation function,' an underdeveloped sense of the reality of his physical here and now. . . . Whatever supervised his sense of physical direction in the external world was only too often just not at home when called upon" (Van der Post, p. 69). The Sun in Leo indicates the intuitive function, and by Jung's definition, that makes sensation the inferior function. "It is not surprising, therefore, that all his life he was to love stone especially and . . . his dialogue with stone took on a more active and outgoing form" (Van der Post, p. 74). Stone is the embodiment of the less conscious earth of the inferior function sensation function.

The "stone" that Jung loved so well was the gift of the unconscious to his Scorpio Midheaven. When he went deep within himself, he found this solid connection to the earth to be sustaining and refreshing. The essence of his psychology is practical too: finding the inner spiritual values is essential to psychological healing. Transformation occurs when we can look at a stone, or a child, or a rainbow, and see the spirit within it.

When Jung began his career as a psychiatrist, solar arc Midheaven was conjunct Mars and solar arc Pluto (ruler of the Midheaven) was semi-sextile Venus

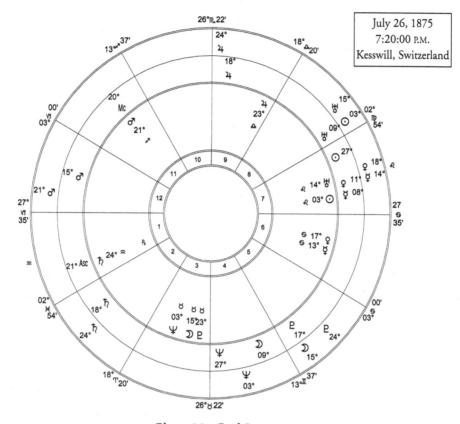

Chart 33. Carl Jung

(ruler of the IC). Ebertin states that these two aspects indicate ego-conscious action and the state of falling in love. Jung fell in love with the idea that the mind was where he would find his place as a healer, and he went into psychiatry fully aware of what he wanted.

He also fell in love with numerous women and was also totally convinced that polygamy was the correct course in life. He evidently allowed the pleasure-seeking Taurus on the IC to become active and succumbed to counter-transference with his patients, both male and female (Noll, p. 87).

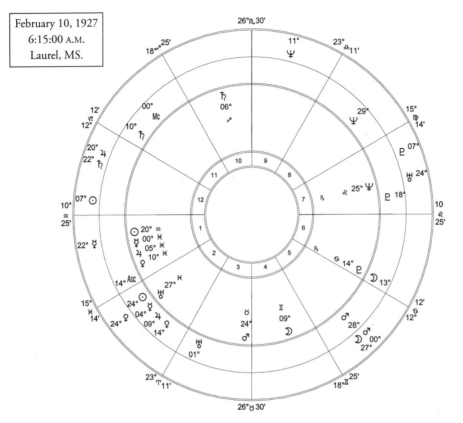

Chart 34. Leontyne Price

Leontyne Price

In 1961 Leontyne Price made her debut at the Metropolitan Opera House (chart 34). Her voice has a brilliance unlike any other soprano. Her rendition of *Aida* is as moving as anything I have ever heard, and earned her reviews as the perfect Aida. Of herself she said, "For a long time, the only time I felt beautiful—complete—as a woman, as a human being—was when I was singing" (Rodden, p. 325).

At the time of her Met debut, Ms. Price has solar arc Midheaven move from Sagittarius into Capricorn to sextile natal Mercury, indicative of ego-conscious activity and advancement in her career through the voice. Solar arc Ascendant trined Pluto (ruler of the Midheaven) while Solar arc Venus (ruler of the IC) squared Pluto, indicating that she had moved into her place of power. By transit Mars opposed the solar arc Midheaven. All this signaled a degree of success that she had perhaps sought, but never attained until then.

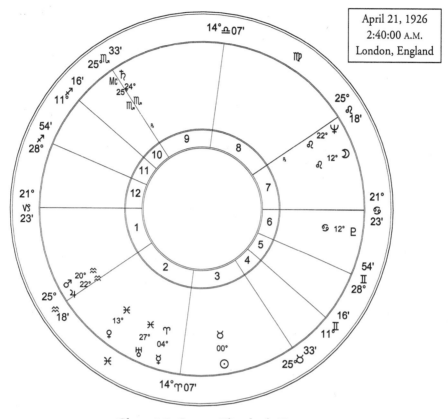

Chart 35. Queen Elizabeth II

It is from the Taurus IC, ruled by Venus, that the power of her profound voice comes. The Scorpio Midheaven indicates the intent of Price's life and the drive that pushed her toward success, but it is the IC, with Mars conjunct, that fuels the voice with energy from deep within the unconscious reaches of mind. She achieved her Met success when transiting Mars reached the opposition to solar arc Midheaven, replicating the natal Mars-Midheaven aspect.

Queen Elizabeth II

Queen Elizabeth II has Saturn exactly conjunct her Midheaven in Scorpio (chart 35). With the benefit of substantial education, both in traditional subject areas and in the politics of statesmanship, she grew up in an environment that emphasized her responsibilities as a member of the royal family. When she took the throne, she stated that she would pursue those responsibilities faithfully and she has, through thick and thin.

The sanity of her Scorpio Midheaven lies in maintaining an aura of reserve amidst the emotionally laden circumstances she encounters. This has no doubt been difficult with Saturn right there provoking her obstinate nature. However, Saturn also works to her advantage, as it reflects her seriousness, her ability to deal with difficult problems, and her capacity for endurance. Her best work requires a serious environment, and her public position does not permit the display of personal emotions (some people probably think she has none, but the Scorpio Midheaven tells us this is not the case). She has the Saturnian strengths of education (ninth house) and restraint (conjunct the Midheaven).

Mars, Jupiter, and Neptune all square the Midheaven, reflecting challenges from multiple sources that she has to face. The close trine of Uranus to the Midheaven sets the condition for sudden surprises that could challenge her own self-esteem. The sesqui-square to Pluto from the sixth house is indicative of the kinds of tension and stress she experiences in her role as monarch.

Other Scorpio Midheavens

Truman Capote, September 30, 1924, 3:00 P.M., New Orleans, Louisiana

Jane Fonda, December 21, 1937, 9:14 A.M., Manhattan, New York

Alexander Ruperti, May 23, 1913, 10:30 P.M., Stuttgart, Germany

Kirk Douglas, December 9, 1916, 10:15 A.M., Amsterdam, New York

Liberace, May 16, 1919, 11:15 P.M., West Allis, Wisconsin

Sophia Loren, September 20, 1934, 2:10 P.M., Rome, Italy

John Hinckley, May 29, 1955, 11:42 P.M., Ardmore, Oklahoma

Prince William, June 21, 1982, 11:03 A.M., London, England

Doris Doane, April 4, 1913, 1:57 A.M., Mansfield, Massachusetts

Billie Jean King, November 22, 1943, 11:45 A.M., Long Beach, California

11

SAGITTARIUS MIDHEAVEN

For individuals born in the Northern Hemisphere, Sagittarius Midheavens form an angle of less than 90 degrees to the Ascendant. This results in a general self-awareness that is consistent with persona. Ascendants associated with Sagittarius Midheavens are Aquarius and Pisces. Those with Aquarius Ascendants will appear to emphasize the process of intellect while those with Pisces rising will appear to use more intuitive processes. In both cases the power of the Sagittarius Midheaven lies in the use of mind to guide the will.

Sagittarius is a mutable fire sign and located in the ninth house in the natural wheel. It is as close to the Midheaven as Capricorn, a sign normally associated with ambition. Sagittarius shares the quality of status-seeking with Capricorn, yet Sagittarius may be somewhat more subtle in this area. This is because the Sagittarius Midheaven is aware of the desire for standing on a conscious level. Sagittarius is able to create plans that include higher standing as a result of some other goal. Thus status is not the main aim of any activity; it is more of a fringe benefit.

Ability to Plan

Sagittarius Midheavens know they have the skill to plan well. The intuitive side of their nature lends itself to seeing how things will develop in the future and

135

provides a direct link between present circumstances and the attainment of future goals. Because Sagittarius is between the desire sign, Scorpio, and the utilization sign, Capricorn, these individuals are in an ideal position to connect with both. They open their minds to any idea which can further their plans. In youth they are susceptible to suggestion from any direction. As they develop discrimination, they evaluate other people's ideas and discard those that do not fit.

While Sagittarius Midheavens can appear arbitrary in their planning process, they actually are considering every idea that crosses their minds. They have developed the introspective process to an art form and use their internal sense of proper direction skillfully. They tend to keep things moving constantly. Unlike earth signs, they don't need to see concrete finished products; they trust the developmental process more. They can go on to the next plan before the current one has reached total maturity.

Conservative Attitude

Sagittarius leads into the heart of the winter season. There is no room for wastefulness in this bleak time of year—Sagittarius Midheavens recognize this basic truth. They know that they are capable of conserving what they have better than any other sign. This ability reflects the wisdom of Jupiter, the ruler. It also reflects the capacity to adapt to current circumstances while keeping one eye on the future.

One result of the conservative attitude is that Sagittarius Midheavens form conclusions about the world which are difficult to shake. They sometimes appear to be very opinionated as a result of this inner certainty. It is not that they are unwilling to change their minds; it is more that they are unwilling to do so without some really good reason. They need to be convinced. They need others to present compelling evidence before they will change their minds. When they change, they adhere to the new idea as completely as they did to the old. This steadfastness is the base for their self-awareness.

Open-Mindedness

Sagittarius Midheavens also know that they can open their minds to any idea without damaging their intellectual structure. They will entertain any bizarre idea for the sake of argument. They may seem to accept your line of thought, when they are actually only considering it. Others make the mistake of thinking they have convinced Sagittarius when they have only been heard. Still, Sagittarius Midheavens allow others to think what they like. They seem dogmatic because they stick to their own decisions, yet they do not require others to adopt their views. This style of thinking can be hard on other signs because they are less flexible.

Spiritual Nature

Sagittarius at the Midheaven reflects a self-awareness that includes strong positions about religion and spiritual matters. These individuals do not always take on a formal religion; however, they often have definite views where religion is concerned. Because Sagittarius takes a firm position and does not change easily, they are sometimes stereotyped for life even thought their positions are not that immutable.

Ignatius Loyola, the founder of the Jesuit order, had strong beliefs about his superior role in the social and political arena. After a serious accident he experienced a conversion which led him to found the order. He did not forget what he knew about the politics and economics of his time. He did not become a meek servant. Rather, he took what he knew and applied it wholeheartedly in his new religious mission. His training and knowledge served his new motives.

Karl Marx, at the other end of the spectrum, denied the validity of religion. He felt that the political system could and should fulfill all the needs of all the people. His *Communist Manifesto* reveals to the reader the boundaries of his beliefs.

Adventurous Nature

Sagittarius Midheavens enjoy adventure. They know that results reflect careful planning, so they plan well. Not the gambler that Leo can be, Sagittarius considers every possibility so that there are very few random variables. Adventure does not mean danger. Rather, it means having fun by engaging in a complex activity and performing it well. I think of an acting teacher who drills her students with voice and body exercises in order to achieve a very natural effect on stage. I think of a dancer who practices hours of steps, but who looks loose and spontaneous in the performance. I think of a hunter who goes into the high mountains in the late fall, prepared for the hunt but also prepared for accidents, bad weather, and any number of other contingencies. Success lies in the planning.

Resistance

Resistance lies between what we have now and what we want to have. Sagittarius Midheavens experience resistance when they want to hold on to their philosophical position as well as include new ideas. They are always looking for a model that accommodates everything they experience because then they don't have to let go, they merely rearrange things. I have found the astrological model to be such. It has a place for every thought, every feeling, every principle. Naturally some take on greater importance, at least for a time, while others fade into the background.

It is a major leap of faith for the Sagittarius Midheaven to adopt a new model of the world. By the same token the new model can be considered, entertained, investigated, and otherwise examined until it has eased itself into the scheme of things. Then it no longer needs to displace something else; it simply absorbs it. The Sagittarius Midheaven student can wake up one morning knowing. They no longer need to believe. This kind of knowing is the strength of Sagittarius Midheavens.

Capacity to Respond

For the Sagittarius Midheaven who has a very broad model of the universe, responding to the needs of others is simple. Such a person determines what needs to be done and then does it, or finds someone to do it. Within their orderly belief system there is plenty of room for such action. For a Sagittarius who has developed a very narrow model, responding is more difficult because the model may not include any responsive components. Such a Sagittarius Midheaven will be in the position to react, not respond, and this can be a serious difficulty.

It becomes clear that for this sign which precedes the winter solstice, defining the self occurs less in terms of human personality and more in terms of higher soul. When Sagittarius Midheavens achieve this level, then they are able to respond easily in both the physical and spiritual realms. Ordinary ambition and direction are replaced by spiritual aspirations. One does not lose his or her material capabilities, but rather focuses all activity in terms of spirit.

Sanity and Neurosis

The three thinking styles associated with Sagittarius at the Midheaven include the following astrological correspondences:

1. The cusp of Scorpio and Sagittarius, or the movement from fixed water to mutable fire.

2. The pure energy of the mutable fire sign itself.

3. The cusp of Sagittarius and Capricorn, or the movement from mutable fire to cardinal earth.

These three relationships describe both the neurotic potential of Sagittarius on
the Midheaven and the sanity to be found there.

Scorpio/Sagittarius Cusp

The neuroses of Sagittarius develop in the intersections between Scorpio, "I
desire," and Capricorn, "I utilize." The transition from Scorpio to Sagittarius
addresses the shift from physical desire to spiritual aspiration. For the Sagittarius
Midheaven, this transition is polarized in this way: it is not that Scorpio cannot
have higher aspirations or that Sagittarius never has lower ones; Sagittarius Midheavens know that they are making this transition. They can identify exactly
where they are in the process. They have desires as intense as anyone else does.
The example charts in this chapter address the desire principle in various ways,
illustrating the levels of philosophical attitude that are possible.

The Pure Energy of Sagittarius at the Midheaven

The second thinking style of the Sagittarius Midheaven deals with the energy of
the pure mutable fire sign. Resting in the energy of Sagittarius reflects the pure
energy of the fire element as it expresses through the mutable quality. The more
interior neurosis of Sagittarius involves what happens when they rest with the void,
the space between their philosophical and spiritual beliefs. One neurotic response
is to feel the terrible pain of loneliness and to seek protection from that pain. Protection is found in consuming and then discarding. In children we see the lust to
own a particular toy and the casual disregard of that toy after it has been used.

Fear is at the foundation of isolation. If we use others only to resolve our own
fear, then we cannot truly connect with them. When we connect with others and
recognize their aloneness, we develop compassion, one of the cornerstones of
awareness. We are able to relate instead of isolating. When we relate in this way
we can drop the total seriousness which grew out of personal pain and take up a
lighter, more humorous stance. We can experience the joy of life.

Sagittarius/Capricorn Cusp

The third thinking style of the Sagittarius Midheaven is concerned with the transition from Sagittarius to Capricorn, or from mutable fire to cardinal earth. The

transition from Sagittarius to Capricorn focuses the Sagittarius Midheaven on the utilization of things. Once an object of desire is attained, the question becomes one of use. The neurotic Sagittarius will use things only to provide relief for his or her own loneliness and pain. When a person or object no longer fulfills that need, it is tossed aside, but not discarded.

If the fear of poverty becomes consuming, Sagittarius Midheavens cannot see themselves as comfortable no matter what they have. The things they own have become identified with who and what they are. They become insecure in themselves because they know that things are ephemeral and they have identified themselves with those things. Hence they doubt themselves. The sanity of the Sagittarius Midheaven lies in the potential of transmutation. When Sagittarius Midheavens find their security in the very truth of impermanence, they then work with the flow of their lives without attachment. They can still have beautiful things around them, but they no longer are identified with the things. Then and only then can the Sagittarius Midheaven experience the limitless wealth to be found in the world of experience.

Summary

The sanity of Sagittarius Midheavens arises when they recognize the capacity for transmutation. They cease to be limited by the desire for material things around them and begin to be concerned about spiritual values. They form human relationships based upon mutual support in reaching toward future objectives together. To do this they draw on the qualities of Gemini, the sign on the IC, as Gemini sees the logic of interrelationships easily, and also understands the nature if impermanence. Finally, they overcome the fear of poverty by relating to spaciousness instead of to the objects that appear to fill the space.

Creativity

Sagittarius Midheavens know they have deep creative wells from which to draw. The understanding of duality as a requisite for material expression provides Sagittarius with the inspiration to work in the physical as well as the spiritual realms. The Jupiter rulership of Sagittarius indicates, on the higher plane, the instrumentality of love-wisdom in all thought and action. Each person is born into a physical body and must learn the true import of the material world: Sagittarius Midheavens know the true relationship between the material and spiritual realms—they can create out of either or both as needed.

Conscious Choice

The freedom to act rests directly on the larger law of the universe for the Sagittarius Midheaven. The deep understanding of aloneness makes relationship to others dependent on decisions of will, not on accident. Sagittarius Midheavens also know that their true motives may not impress others. Hence they may not reveal their inner thoughts. They will describe their ambition in terms that other people can understand, and they are often very convincing. Even people who disagree with their decisions eventually must applaud their steadfastness and logic. Will, for the Sagittarius Midheaven, is an instrument to achieve and maintain balance between the desire path in the physical world and a path of aspiration in the spiritual world.

Free will, for Sagittarius Midheavens, emerges from the compassion underlying the desire of Scorpio, the wisdom found in Sagittarius energy, and the humanity found in the earthy energy of Capricorn. Will can be used to satisfy personal desire and it can be used to utilize people and things for personal gain, or it can also be directed toward spiritual desires—aspirations on a different level. When compassion for others enters into the equation, will is engaged in the service of a larger world. At this point, the loneliness the Sagittarius Midheaven knows so well is transmuted into action.

Spiritual Growth

The Sagittarius Midheaven transmutes desire into spiritual aspiration when the constant cycle of desire, acquisition, and discarding stops. Enlightenment occurs when goals become part of a process of development and not end results. When attachment to things and ideas ceases to be the end goal, then enlightenment is possible. The self-aware Sagittarius Midheaven knows the pure joy of the generous act—an act that we do not have to do, but which we freely choose to do. When the Sagittarius Midheaven finds the center of being in mind, enlightenment occurs.

Ivan the Terrible

Ivan the Terrible exemplifies the Sagittarius Midheaven, conscious of both physical desires and spiritual aspirations (chart 36). "Nervous, passionate, easily excited, and incapable of concealing his emotions, Ivan as a child showed many

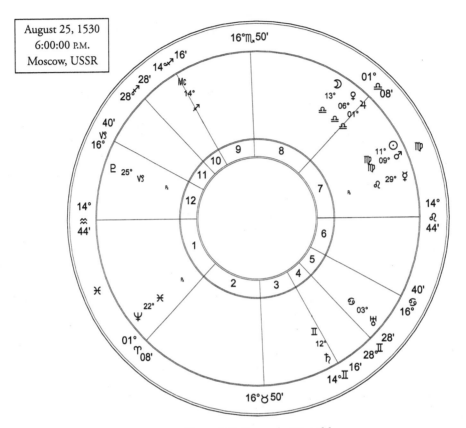

August 25, 1530
6:00:00 P.M.
Moscow, USSR

Chart 36. Ivan the Terrible

of the characteristics he would reveal later. He was fascinated by church rituals, pilgrimages, sacred relics . . . he learned long passages of the Scriptures by heart" (Payne, p. 35). This statement about Ivan exemplifies the Sagittarius Midheaven, conscious of both physical desires and spiritual aspirations.

"From his childhood he had known nothing but coups and countercoups, intrigues, treachery, the great princes continually attempting to seize power by surprise attacks on the Kremlin, by murder or by stealth. Sensitive, widely read, with knowledge of political affairs far in advance of his years, Ivan was well aware of the dangers of his high position. Many of the tragedies of his reign have their source in his childhood fears and childhood terrors" (Payne, p. 43). Ivan fell prey to both the political intrigue around him and to the fears of the less conscious Sagittarius-Gemini axis.

He committed his first murder at age thirteen. After that he beat and robbed people in the streets, threw dogs off balconies to their death, and generally terrorized Moscow. Five or six years later he would compose hymns to be sung in parts. Clearly the two sides of his mind were at war with each other.

On the day of his coronation, solar arc Midheaven moved from Sagittarius into Capricorn and squared Jupiter. Solar arc Saturn sextiled natal Mercury, ruler of the IC, reflecting his distrust of others and his narrow-minded view of the world. Transits included Uranus semi-square the Midheaven, Saturn square Jupiter, ruler of the Midheaven, and Jupiter sesqui-square Jupiter. As the directed Midheaven moved into Capricorn, his position served to move Ivan from a person at least somewhat interested in spiritual matters to a being focused on attainment of his objectives. He became more and more isolated within his own mind after this date. The transits indicate the great stress he experienced at the time of the coronation, and demonstrated throughout the rest of his life.

Allen Ginsberg

Allen Ginsberg's poetry reflects the depth of self-awareness he developed throughout his life (chart 37) (www.charm.net/~brooklyn/People/Allen Ginsberg.html and www.charm.net/~brooklyn/Poems/Howl.html). From a childhood marred by his Russian mother's insanity, he retained the thoughts and feelings that went into "Kaddish" and "White Shroud," two of his best poems. His profound understanding of her suffering was coupled with Buddhist precepts of the four noble truths and became a foundation piece of his work.

Jupiter, ruler of the Midheaven, sextiles it from the twelfth house. Also in the twelfth, the Moon forms a quintile to the Midheaven. These two planets focus on Ginsberg's private life as the driver of his poetry. His immersion in Buddhist meditation made it possible for him to write about life and death "from the heart," and his presence was warm and compassionate. His poetry provides the basis for a rationale for dropping out of the political culture of the United States and addresses the intense pain Ginsberg saw all around him. He begins "Howl" by saying:

> *I saw the best minds of my generation destroyed by madness,*
> *starving hysterical naked.*

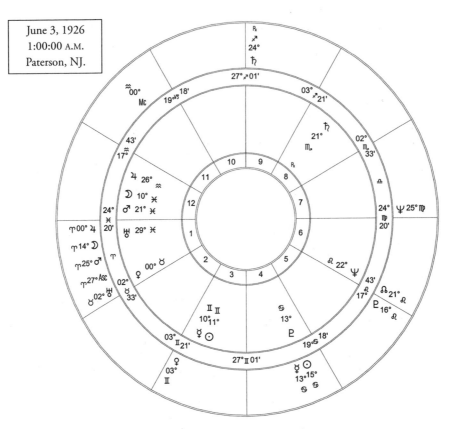

June 3, 1926
1:00:00 A.M.
Paterson, NJ.

Chart 37. Allen Ginsberg

Then he captures the beauty and joy of life in "Sunflower Sutra":

Look at the sunflower, he said . . .
I rushed up enchanted—it was my first sunflower . . .
We're not our skin of grime, we're not our dread bleak dusty imageless locomotive,
we're all beautiful golden sunflowers inside, we're blessed by our own seed & golden
hairy naked accomplishment-bodies

At the time he published "Kaddish," a poem for his mother on the anniversary
of her death, Ginsberg had solar arc Mars sextiling Jupiter, ruler of the Midheaven. Jupiter had moved by solar arc to 0 degrees of Aries, reflecting the release
of creative energy and the growth of self-awareness. The Midheaven had moved
to 0 degrees of Aquarius and squared Venus, indicating that Ginsberg himself

was the agent for the production of this poetic statement, even though it followed the death of his mother and could be thought to be an outgrowth if his reaction to that event. The solar arc Ascendant was trine the Midheaven, indicating that he brought his persona to his writing—his persona was essential to his self-awareness at that time. These auspicious shifts reflect the moment in which Ginsberg wrote what many consider to be his best work. They clearly reflect the possibility for transmutation of feelings and beliefs that pervade Ginsberg's writing.

Elisabeth Kübler-Ross

Elisabeth Kübler-Ross has done more to change our attitudes toward death and treatment for the dying than any other single individual (chart 38). Her work focused on individuals who were dying, but provided a model for the stages of the grieving process that can be applied to many of life's situations. While not everyone agrees with her mapping of the grief process, her work remains the foundation of many academic programs that teach about work with the dying and the bereaved.

A childhood illness may have been the spark for her later work. She told her hospital roommate that she was going to the other side. She said she saw angels waiting for her (Kübler-Ross, p. 29). Her life work strove to bring the peace of mind to people in the moment of death, and to those left behind. She had a vision of what the end is like, and she made it her mission to help others who lacked that clear insight.

A second incident occurred when she was about fifty-two years old. She was bitten by a spider and became seriously ill as a result. Among numerous aspects indicating the severity of the crisis, solar arc Midheaven trined Venus in the third house and opposed Mercury in the sixth house, and Jupiter, ruler of the Midheaven, squared the North node in the fifth. The combined self-awareness concerned the ending of life (fourth house), openness to the work of communicating her knowledge (sixth house), and associations (North Node) involved in the creative process (fifth house), served to spark her future work and to fuel it with profound insight into suffering. She grasped the truth of impermanence. It was her ability to understand death without identifying with it that makes her work such a gift to humanity.

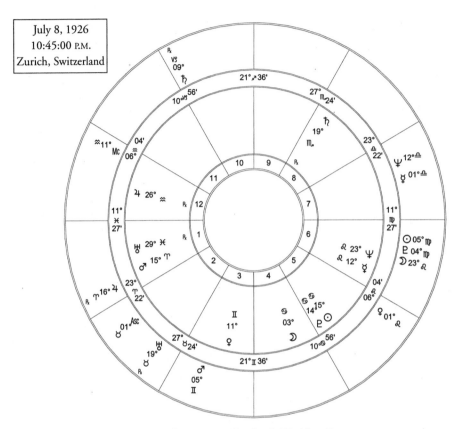

Chart 38. Elisabeth Kübler-Ross

Other Sagittarius Midheavens

Edward R. Murrow, April 25, 1908, 2:00 A.M., Greensboro, North Carolina

Evel Knievel, October 17, 1938, 2:40 P.M., Butte, Montana

William Shatner, March 22, 1931, 4:00 A.M., Montreal, Quebec

Diahann Carroll, July 17, 1935, 9:35 P.M., New York, New York

Karl Marx, May 5, 1818, 2:00 A.M., Trier, Germany

James Hoffa, February 14, 1913, 6:52 A.M., Brazil, Indiana

Evangeline Adams, February 8, 1868, 8:30 A.M., Jersey City, New Jersey

Carol Burnett, April 26, 1933, 4:00 A.M., San Antonio, Texas

Audrey Hepburn, May 4, 1929, 3:00 A.M., Brussels, Belgium

Margaret Chase Smith, December 14, 1897, 11:30 A.M., Skowhegan, Maine

12

CAPRICORN MIDHEAVEN

When the Midheaven is 0 degrees Capricorn, the Ascendant is 0 degrees Aries. In the Northern Hemisphere the larger the degree of Capricorn on the Midheaven, the wider the angle between Midheaven and Ascendant. This is because the Ascendant changes more than one degree for each degree the Capricorn Midheaven moves. The rate of speed depends on birth latitude. If all other factors are balanced, the Capricorn Midheaven will respond to the environment to a greater degree and depend less on personal initiative.

Personal interest and ambition drive Capricorn, so responsiveness will not be an obvious personal characteristic. Remember that if the Capricorn Midheaven is further from the Ascendant, this places the Cancer Nadir closer. Thus the inner well of information from the personal and collective minds is focused on nurturing characteristics. Ambitious Capricorns have, at the foundation of their thinking, the urge to care for others. The charts in this chapter address the range of activities that have this internal desire at their base.

Self-Confidence
Capricorn Midheavens know their level of self-confidence. They know what they can accomplish and they believe they can do more. Sure-footed as the mountain

goat, they tread on uneven ground with assurance that they can manage whatever situation arises. Not the type to demand solutions instantly, they can tolerate painful periods during which they hang on to their beliefs and forge ahead. For Capricorn Midheavens, authority grows out of the practical fact that they are accurate in their decisions, careful and economical in their work, and fair in their judgments nearly all the time. Were they not, they would have little or no authority. All these capabilities contribute to their self-confidence. Capricorn Midheavens know what they have learned and how that knowledge will serve them.

Concentration on Their Own Work

Capricorn Midheavens take themselves and their work very seriously. They often close out other people in order to maintain this one-pointed focus, causing others to believe that they do not care. This is only the appearance; the Cancer IC is always at work internally, monitoring direction in terms of significant others. Still, Capricorn can assume that others understand their motives when there is no outer evidence to demonstrate the longer-range goals.

The positive side of this focus is the astonishing accomplishments of Capricorn Midheavens. They don't just believe they can do things, they *know* they can. This knowing is as powerful as money and position. Some Capricorn Midheavens focus on their own accomplishments, never intending to include others. Some of them have the intention of affecting the whole world, or a large part of it, with their personal work. Some have a bulldozer management style while others appear to allow personal initiative to guide their employees. Many acquire a large following of devoted fans. Knowing they can is indeed at least half the battle for Capricorn Midheavens.

Striving to Obtain Objectives

Capricorn Midheavens do not set goals only to fall short. They set goals in order to attain them. When obstacles appear, they surmount them, never giving up until they cannot move at all. Some Capricorn Midheavens have to be dead to be stopped, like Robert Kennedy, Martin Luther King, Jr., and Amelia Earhart. Some are forced to reassess their goals and change direction. Some, like Teresa of Avila, take a contemplative path because they feel the strength of the Cancer Nadir driving them to manifest their devotion. The common thread is accomplishment.

Ego-Consciousness Through Endurance

Capricorn Midheavens gain self-awareness through endurance. They keep going and keep going, long after others have faltered. Somewhere in the struggle they become aware of themselves. It certainly does not happen when they are inactive because they are so seldom without a project. It happens in the midst of the work. Capricorn Midheavens demonstrate the essence of karma yoga in that they place their faith in the work itself and not in the individuals who do the work.

Capricorn Midheavens raise their work to an art form when they convince others of its significance. After 175 years we are still reading Byron's poetry; Martin Luther King, Jr. convinced Americans of the need for civil rights legislation; Annie Besant brought attention to the theosophical movement; Elvis Presley was a legend during his own lifetime and he changed the course of popular music. Examples only serve to confirm that Capricorn Midheavens know the importance of their work, both personally and globally.

Simple and Modest

Ebertin says Capricorn Midheavens are simple and modest. Here is an example of the importance of understanding any quality as part of a continuum. When I look at the list of famous people who have this Midheaven, at first I doubt that they are simple *or* modest. Then it becomes clear that the individuals are not the source of their own fame; it is their followers who create the glamour around them. The followers are directed unconsciously to the Cancer Nadir; they are aware of the well of insistent energy that drives Capricorn Midheavens and they bring that into the light. Teresa of Avila certainly had a simple life; Elvis might have fared better if he had sought more simplicity and modesty in his daily activities.

Prosaic Nature

Prosaic means "characteristic of prose as distinguished from poetry." On one end of the spectrum we find Byron and Shelley, poets of great skill. On the other end we find ordinary people who go from day to day accomplishing their work without fanfare. We find the whole range in between of people who have a flair for the dramatic and those who do most of their work alone. Capricorn Midheavens do not fulfill the definition of prosaic if that definition includes "dull and unimaginative." They do fulfill the definition of "everyday," in the sense that they make an effort each day—high quality work becomes the ordinary expectation.

Sense of Reality

Capricorn Midheavens have a sense of reality that guides them. They know what will work and they know what they are getting themselves into when they take on a cause. Joan Baez and Martin Luther King, Jr. knew they risked jail time and even their own lives when they took on the issues of nonviolence and civil rights. Robert Kennedy knew also. Capricorn Midheavens know themselves and what they can accomplish. They know they do not control the entire world, yet they exercise power through their ideas, and they use that power to achieve their goals.

Growth of the Inner Spiritual Nature

While Capricorn Midheavens are engaged in outer expressions of productivity, they are also developing their spiritual awareness. The very experience of manipulating the material world places Capricorn in an ideal position to make progress in understanding the soul. Nowhere is it clearer that intelligent activity includes a search for meaning and that meaning is to be found in spiritual pursuits. Capricorn Midheavens have developed the capacity for intense effort on the physical plane; they know that they carry this effort over into the spiritual realm throughout their lives.

Resistance

Nothing seems as resistant as a stubborn Capricorn Midheaven. I have heard astrologers call Capricorn "the only fixed cardinal sign." This joking appellation comes from experiencing the immovable determination of Capricorn to accomplish the goal. Resistance is the space between what one has and what one wants. Do Capricorn Midheavens experience this? It seems that the resistance is like stone: it only is relieved when the stone has turned to dust under the pressure of desire. Capricorn Midheavens may resist relaxation and rest more than anything else.

Capacity to Respond

Capricorn Midheavens respond from a practical position. Their first instinct is to do what works in a given situation and this is generally an acceptable response. They may take a very short view of the problem, however. What will work best for the next ten minutes may not be what is best in the long run. The more cultivated Capricorn response is to allow events to unfold, interfering as little as possible while maintaining some kind of control. They seek to function in terms of intelligent activity rather than reacting from feelings which will change with the tide of activity. Also, by not responding too solidly, they leave openings for change to occur.

Sanity and Neurosis

The three thinking styles associated with Aquarius at the Midheaven include the following astrological correspondences:

1. The cusp of Sagittarius and Capricorn, or the movement from mutable fire to cardinal earth.

2. The pure energy of the cardinal earth sign itself.

3. The cusp of Capricorn and Aquarius, or the movement from cardinal earth to fixed air.

These three relationships describe both the neurotic potential of Aquarius on the Midheaven and the sanity to be found there.

Sagittarius/Capricorn Cusp

The movement from a fire sign to an earth sign, in Buddhist psychology, is connected with expanded awareness. The neurotic expression of this kind of awareness is suppressed feeling. This is not the same as repression, wherein feelings are buried in the unconscious and kept there by unconscious processes. Suppression is a conscious decision to avoid painful feelings. It is an attempt to deal with situations objectively rather than expressing one's true condition. There is a fear that such a revelation will be too painful to tolerate. The mind becomes rigid in its attempt to avoid feelings.

The sanity that relates to this neurosis is creative self-control. Capricorn Midheavens can make creative personal decisions in dealing with feelings. When Capricorn Midheavens allow themselves to have feelings, they enrich their presence in the world and they respond to others more authentically. The resulting openness allows them to have the positive feelings that they have been suppressing along with those they perceived to be negative.

The Pure Energy of Capricorn at the Midheaven

The second Capricorn thinking style deals with a rigid mind. Capricorn Midheavens need to perceive the openness of space around them; when mind becomes overly rigid, the spaciousness seems to disappear, producing a feeling of solid walls and no pathways. The resulting feelings include suspicion, pessimism, and selfishness, all designed to protect the psyche from the trapped feelings.

The sanity side of this neurosis lies in awareness of openness. Even the rigidity usually leads to surrender to the truth of self-awareness. Capricorn Midheavens know the difference between concentration of energy and limitation. They are generally able to work with the practical side of life without submerging in unattractive feelings. And when they do indulge in feelings, they are generally able to master them by exercising self-control. The greater the potential for openness at every level, the more fully Capricorn Midheavens can understand themselves and the polarities that drive them.

Capricorn/Aquarius Cusp

The third Capricorn thinking style is reflected in the transition from cardinal earth to fixed air. In alchemy the earth air transition has a practical down-to-earth quality balanced by a logical perspective. The destructive thinking of this pattern comes from the fear of limitation. Capricorn Midheavens always want to have multiple avenues open to them and feel trapped when choices are not readily identifiable. They also may get caught in the dilemma of how to deal with situations in which all choices seem to be undesirable. Self-aware Capricorn Midheavens know that occasionally they will have to make do with unpalatable choices. They depend on their skills and intelligent activity to make the best of such difficulties. Intelligent activity includes looking ahead to see what is there. Capricorns usually have one eye on the road ahead and one on potential problems. Their prudent systematic approach to life avoids the kind of crises one expects from more careless signs.

Creativity

Capricorn Midheavens know that their creativity arises from a deep well of feeling, even though they seldom reveal those feelings. With Cancer at the Nadir, the well consists of the natural flow of energies throughout systems. In the case of Capricorn at the Midheaven, the flow comes through the psyche from the collective and personal unconscious, emerging in the form of Capricornian activity.

A casual observer would not recognize the source—only the results would be apparent. Even the Capricorn Midheaven might deny the depth of the source. In times of intense personal crisis the power of feeling emerges directly, making everyone aware that the Capricorn Midheaven is human after all.

Conscious Choice

The key phrase, "I utilize," describes the way in which Capricorn Midheavens mobilize free will. These individuals are placed in the world to use material things. They create environments for others and for themselves out of whatever they find. They may not be entirely fair about what they appropriate for their own use; they may not even care about being fair. However, they do not waste materials. They are conservative in their use as well, not demanding too much of each object in their world. One problem is that other people may be treated as objects instead of people. While Capricorn Midheavens may not mean to mistreat others, their demanding nature does not engender respect from others. Capricorn Midheavens are more successful when they find effective ways to reward their associates. They are most successful when they are able to motivate others rather without making demands.

Spiritual Growth

Capricorn Midheavens are more confident when they see the results of careful work. They make plans and execute them, hoping for productive outcomes, and when a project is completed, Capricorns can see, manifested in the physical world, the results of their effort. By acknowledging the fountain of creative energy coming from the sign of Cancer at the IC, Capricorn Midheavens realize their potential for spiritual growth. There is no room for arrogance here. Only through humility can Capricorn Midheavens discover their true role as servants of humanity. By the same token, they must conquer the physical world in order to triumph in the spiritual realm. When worldly ambition is refocused on the desire for spiritual wealth, Capricorn Midheavens become enlightened.

Percy Bysshe Shelley

To Shelley, freedom meant license to do or say whatever he wished, without much care for others (chart 39). He borrowed freely and was in debt much of his life. The fact that he was terrorized by his classmates at Eton and called "Mad Shelley" did nothing to quell an already volatile temperament. It fostered in him

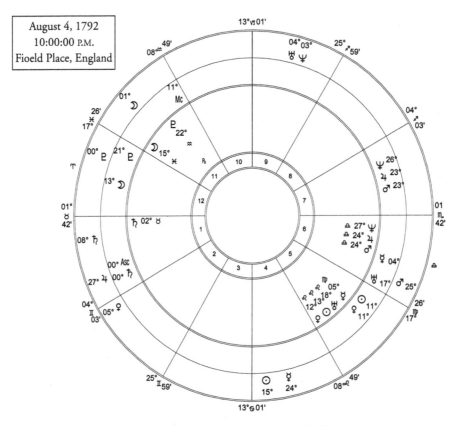

Chart 39. Percy Bysshe Shelley

a fear and hatred of authority that was reflected in his radical political views and libertine lifestyle. He was plagued by nightmares and sleepwalking throughout his life.

He could be possessed of a singular arrogance. His correspondence contains numerous instances in which he ripped into his target, stating all of that person's weaknesses and shortcomings. When he had finished, he then asked that person to send him his belongings, or to loan him money.

A few months after he left his wife Harriet and eloped with Mary, he wrote an especially arrogant letter to Harriet. "He told her that he would have liked to have 'superintended' the progress of her mind, and have assisted her in 'cultivating an elevated philosophy'. He was broadly dismissive. 'I am united to another; you are no longer my wife.' In a postscript Shelley states that he is confident

Harriet can manage the impending birth of a child without him and then closed "by asking her to send on to Hookham 'stockings, hanks and Mrs. Wollstonecraft's posthumous works.'" (Holmes, p. 255).

When you consider Capricorn at the Midheaven, you must, in this case, conclude that Shelley was largely unconscious of his motivations. He was often selfish and materialistic, unsympathetic to the needs or desires of others, all Capricorn traits. He also demonstrated some of the best and worst of Cancer at the IC: brooding dreamy, even mediumistic, immersed in the feelings that gave rise to his poetry.

Shelley's Midheaven formed a sextile to the Moon (reflecting depth of feelings and an appreciation of spiritual values). On the downside, this aspect to the ruler of the IC indicates opportunities to form close relationships with women, each of which he billed as a spiritual connection, but which was usually short lived. The Midheaven also was quincunx the Sun, Venus, and Uranus in the fifth house, indicating that his creative process was subject to the broad mood swings and shifting consciousness of his objectives, an eternal falling in love with new partners, and severe upsets due to his reckless behavior. These aspects also account for his emotional tension and vision, two factors that illuminate his writing.

Shelley was an *enfant terrible* who died a month prior to his thirtieth birthday without the opportunity to mellow with age. At the time of his death, he was willfully sailing into a severe storm and would not lower the sails on his small craft. He had been having visions that were terrifying, and the day before his death he remarked that he felt he had lived as long as his father. The solar arc Midheaven opposed Venus and the Moon, ruler of the IC, trined the Sun. He probably felt that he would either triumph over the storm or not, as destiny would have it. Additional aspects included solar arc Saturn ruler of the Midheaven moving into the sign of Gemini and solar arc Uranus forming a sesquisquare to Saturn, indicative of both the inner agitation which he felt and the nature of the storm in which he drowned.

Genghis Khan and Geraldine Ferraro

Genghis Kahn (chart 40) and Geraldine Ferraro (chart 41) may share their Midheavens in early degrees of Capricorn, but the course of their political lives took very different directions. Orphaned at age ten, Temujin was given the name we

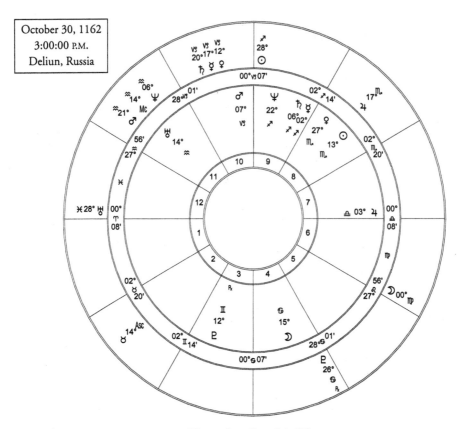

Chart 40. Genghis Khan

know him by when he united the Mongols in 1206. Genghis Khan means *universal ruler*. His success was gained through his organized military, the mobility lent by horses, and his own capacity to devise strong strategies. While he never learned to read, he was able to take existing codes of law and forge them into a workable system.

At the time he came to power, Genghis Khan had solar arc Midheaven conjunct his birth Uranus and solar are Moon trine the birth Midheaven. The Midheaven aspect to Uranus reflects his ability to strike at the right moment and to galvanize warring factions into one unit through the sheer force of his will and personality. The Moon aspect to the Midheaven indicates the condition of his emotional side. It suggests that his goals were deeply rooted in his being. We can assume that the influence of women came into his lie in a big way, but that never deterred him from pursuing his conquests.

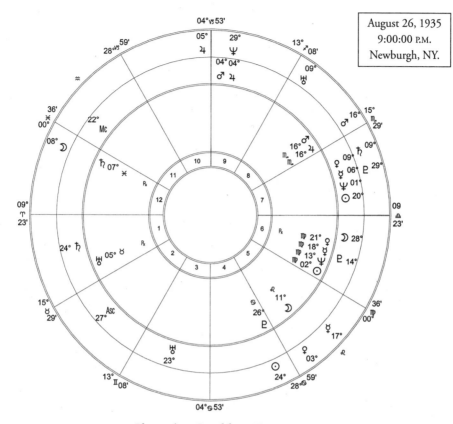

Chart 41. Geraldine Ferraro

Geraldine Ferraro, the first woman to become a vice presidential candidate on a major political ticket in the United States, had a successful political career in Congress. When Walter Mondale chose her as his running mate in 1984, many felt this was a watershed event, reflecting positive change in American politics. She supported economic fairness for women in employment, tax credits for parents who were paying tuition for their children, and she opposed mandatory school busing.

At the time of the nomination, she had Jupiter and Mars conjunct the Midheaven by solar arc, with transiting Jupiter just past the Midheaven, suggesting a pinnacle in her political career. Unfortunately, at the time that transiting Mars conjuncted her Saturn (ruler of the Midheaven), charges of suspicious real estate deals and her husband's alleged connection to the Mafia came to light. Many

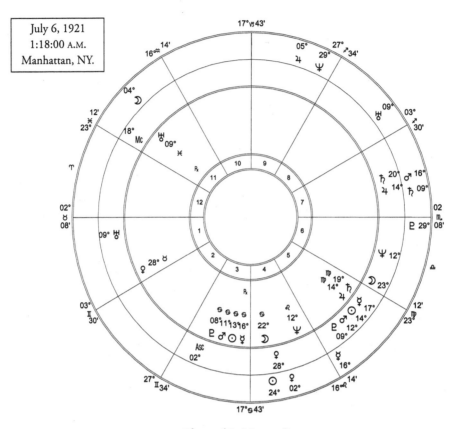

July 6, 1921
1:18:00 A.M.
Manhattan, NY.

Chart 42. Nancy Reagan

perceived these attacks to be anti-Italian. In hindsight we can conclude that these issues were not laid to rest in August, but followed the campaign and probably played a large role in the eventual defeat of the Mondale Ferraro ticket. On October 11 transiting Saturn entered her eighth house and on the twelfth Mars conjuncted the Midheaven. Unlike Genghis Khan, who was able to grasp his opportunities firmly and use his self-awareness to advantage, Ferraro and her candidacy were brought up short through the alleged actions of her husband and through negative campaigning by Republicans. In 1992 she was unsuccessful in a bid for nomination by the Democratic Party for the New York Senate seat, and bowed out of politics.

Nancy Reagan

Although not a candidate herself, Nancy Reagan was prominent in the campaign as well (chart 42). In many ways she typified the perfect wife of the candidate, but later events have shown her to be a tough politician as well. She was able to guide White House activities and influence her President husband as well as anyone in recent times. At the time of the nomination Nancy's solar arc Ascendant was opposite the Midheaven, providing great self-awareness through her own personality, and reflecting the fact that her personality could shine in the light of a national campaign. With no detrimental aspects involving the Midheaven, she was able to move into a position of great power by using her personality to support her husband. Thus she was able to gain the supportive role where Geraldine Ferraro failed.

Other Capricorn Midheavens

Kurt Cobain, September 20, 1967, 7:20 P.M., Aberdeen, Washington

Rose Kennedy, July 22, 1890, 10:00 P.M., Boston, Massachusetts

Nostradamus, December 14, 1503, 12:01 P.M., St. Remy, France

William "Wild Bill" Cody, February 26, 1846, 8:00 A.M., Le Claire, Iowa

Lee Iacocca, October 15, 1924, 5:00 P.M., Allentown, Pennsylvania

Hedda Hopper, May 2, 1885, 4:00 A.M., Hollidaysburg, Pennsylvania

Bette Midler, December 1, 1945, 2:19 P.M., Honolulu, Hawaii

Rabindranath Tagore, May 7, 1861, 4:02 A.M., Calcutta, India

Amelia Earhart, July 24, 1897, 11:30 P.M., Atchison, Kansas

13

AQUARIUS
MIDHEAVEN

When Aquarius falls at the Midheaven in the Northern Hemisphere, the distance between the Midheaven and the Ascendant can be very great. At the Equator the distance is about 95 degrees. This distance increases to about 105 degrees at 30 degrees of latitude, 112 degrees at 40 degrees latitude, and over 150 degrees at 60 degrees of latitude! In the Southern Hemisphere the range is from about 85 degrees down to 39 degrees. This would suggest a wide range of expression, and that is indeed what we find. Responding to outside influences is balanced if there are several planets in the eastern portion of the chart, as the energy of these planets will be experienced as assertive tendencies within the personality.

Aquarius is a fixed air sign. On the Midheaven it indicates an individual who desires to fulfill the key phrase, "I know." While the Sun sign Aquarius may say, "I know," the person with the Aquarius Midheaven has to prove to him or herself that this is be true. Such an individual would say, "I know that I know." No single insult is greater to the Aquarius Midheaven than being called stupid, and no single lifetime work is more important than learning, so that the statement "I know" is completely true. The stubborn drive to achieve the all-knowing position can become a drive that surpasses all others.

Such a person will be a good guest, able to converse on many subjects, able to see the good in almost any situation, and able to find creative choices in the most difficult circumstances. The downside is that nobody likes a know-it-all, so they may try to cover up this tendency, while also covering up any errors that would reveal a lack of knowledge.

The problem with becoming all-knowing is that the Aquarius Midheaven may lose the capacity to discriminate about what should be known. There may also be an inability to discriminate gossip and innuendo from useful information. Sometimes the individual will be better off not cluttering up the consciousness with facts that have little or nothing to do with the work at hand. The same can be said for complete investigation of the unconscious. It is important to remember that we repress things that are too painful to bear, and we forget things that are apparently useless, and such facts may be better left in the unconscious, as long as they are not causing any difficulty.

For the Aquarius Midheaven, then, it may be important to prioritize knowledge. Astrology provides a natural guide through aspects formed by the Midheaven to planets in the natal chart. Through examination of these aspects the astrologer can assess the individual tendency to attain knowledge, and by evaluating the planets, the astrologer can suggest more creative and constructive uses of this drive. The key phrase then becomes "I know what I know, and I seek only what I need to know."

Awareness of the World

The Aquarius Midheaven has the capacity to master the art of awareness. By the same token this Midheaven can lack precision and miss the key point of a discussion. The confident individual knows that observation of the details of events and nuances of feeling are givens for skillful management. You also would know where such abilities break down. With experience the Aquarius Midheaven reaches the point where paying attention is trained into the body. They are always on point in stressful situation, making keen observations for later use.

Attention on the Outcome

The Aquarius Midheaven can assess the capacity for new ideas and the progressive steps involved in effective planning. The best expression of this energy includes the ability to choose from among various strategies and tactics and to predict the results with accuracy. A less developed or younger person may make missteps by neglecting significant details that influence outcomes. If the psyche is burdened with worry or fear, the capacity to gather information may become restricted, and resulting decisions less predictable. The individual will be able to avoid conditions that do not draw upon personal strengths, or find other people who have the requisite skills. The balanced Aquarius Midheaven does not fear failure, but develops contingency plans to provide for unexpected developments. Aquarius, ruled by Uranus, knows that not all outcomes can be planned, and accepts the turns of fortune that could not be anticipated.

Timing

Timing, for the Aquarius Midheaven, is a key factor to the smooth execution of a good plan. When the intuition is cooking, timing is second nature. The individual simply knows when to take action. Other people may wonder why you wait so long, but you know when the moment comes. When the flow slows to a trickle, this fixed sign can demonstrate patience. When things are flying by at light speed, just going with it is challenging, but Aquarius can manage, sorting out the details later. The key lies in jumping on the ride at the right time, the persistence in hanging on (or waiting for the ride to arrive), and balance with the psyche to allow for changes along the way.

When other people feel that operations have gotten off track, the Aquarius Midheaven can discern the subtle new directions as they develop. This is done by focusing on what is actually happening, rather than thinking about or judging what is going wrong. What looks like a dead stop may only be the pause that refreshes. When a raging flood of activity develops, Aquarius can observe from the bank, or at least from the shallow water, so to speak.

Relationships

The Aquarius Midheaven focuses on cooperation with others. Even when the individual is in the executive position, the goal is cooperation, not just supervision. This leadership style tends to allow others to do their best work, intervening occasionally when the situation demands it. Periods of intense personal creativity are balanced by more relaxed, consistent action. There is a strong interest in whatever is new or different, and the Aquarius Midheaven may grasp the essence of a new trend and be willing to work with it long before others see the potential value. The key to success lies in the ability to follow trends on a global scale, while attending to the individual needs of one's immediate associates.

Beyond the shifting economic and political spheres, social roles are constantly changing as well. The Aquarius Midheaven, having developed a flexible attitude toward others, will be able to tolerate a wide range of behaviors, and will be able to enter into new personal social roles as well. The self-aware Aquarius can admit to not knowing everything about a fresh situation. A less conscious individual may follow every fad without discrimination or make firm plans without first testing the overall direction of change.

Resistance

The significant evidence that the Aquarius Midheaven has been weighing since early childhood pivots around the key phrase "I know." As a child you are encouraged to learn, and rewarded for good grades and other evidence of intelligence. If this knowing is allowed to become "knowing best," the mind rigidly attaches to getting its own way. Each thought becomes the best thought, and the ego holds on to it more tightly than the previous one. By holding on, the ego prevents awareness of the present moment.

This is a self-perpetuating cycle. Any new information is mobilized in the battle to be right; if it doesn't fit the pattern, the new idea is discarded, forgotten, or repressed. There is little or no room for incompatible information. Because we cannot know for sure what will happen when we entertain a new idea, and because we are resisting any change in a status quo that we have determined through experience is "right," we rely on past experience and refuse to learn.

Occasionally an event of such magnitude occurs that the Aquarius Midheaven must take notice. If the ego mechanism is rigidly resisting the fresh emotional input, the tried and true behavior is strangely inappropriate for the new situation, but the individual has no alternative. The reactive behavior was successful in protecting the personality in the past, and it is engaged in the new situation whether or not it has any chance of being effective. The reactive behavior is shallow for the very reason that it is designed to avoid looking deeply into the self for answers. If I don't look too deeply, I will not see the fact that I don't really know what to do. I am able to grasp at a tried and true behavior instead of thinking my way through a problem.

Sanity and Neurosis

The three thinking styles associated with Aquarius at the Midheaven include the following astrological correspondences:

1. The cusp of Capricorn and Aquarius, or the movement from cardinal earth to fixed air.

2. The pure energy of the fixed air sign itself.

3. The cusp of Aquarius and Pisces, or the movement from fixed air to mutable water.

These three relationships describe both the neurotic potential of Aquarius on the Midheaven and the sanity to be found there.

Capricorn/Aquarius Cusp

The movement from an earth sign to an air sign is the dynamic in Buddhist psychology of effective action. The movement from cardinal earth to fixed air is the movement from the ambitious formation of practical plans to the steady thought involved in the execution of those plans. This movement employs grounded practical tactics to develop the plan, but may become somewhat less grounded in the execution. Thus the Aquarius Midheaven demands that the individual understand the mechanism that by its nature tends to remove the solid ground. Such an individual will do well to find a career that places steady consistent intellect at a premium. A job where persistence leads to success will draw upon the most skillful means in the individual's array of training and experience.

The neurotic expression of the first thinking style is the doubt about permanence. The perception is that there is solid ground in the beginning, and that the ground will become less solid or even disappear as soon as the individual gets moving. As the neurotic pattern takes root, the individual begins to fear just about everything. Only short-term goals are meaningful because there is no faith that you will be around for anything long-term. There is also a strong focus on the self. First, I need to expect manipulation by others and defend myself against it at all costs. Second, there has to be something in it for me, and right now, because I may not be around to see the future benefits of today's actions. These neurotic worries defeat the expectation of effective action and they prevent objective evaluation of situations, thus causing great harm.

As with all signs, only a small adjustment is needed to turn these neurotic behaviors into a more constructive style. The survival mechanism of Aquarius lies in identifying manipulation by others and seeing it for what it is. The resources for this awareness lie in the opposite sign Leo, where we can define the intuitive capacity of the Aquarius Midheaven. Leo's natural leadership ability is grounded on the ability to discriminate the motives of others from their speech and action. Leo can be either noble or contemptuous in its assessments, and the Aquarius Midheaven can experience either of these intuitively. The best way for Aquarius, or any sign, to manifest intuition creatively is to be clear in its own knowledge. Because of highly developed thinking processes, the Aquarius Midheaven can usually outthink a manipulator. With a benevolent motivation and a strong sense of timing, the Aquarius Midheaven can learn to intervene in the manipulation and turn it to a more effective path. Certainty of the outcome is not even necessary. Certainty lies in the knowledge that you are skilled in identifying the purpose in another person's actions, building on that intention, and redirecting the energy in a way that fulfills a more creative purpose. In other words, you use the impulse of the other individual to accomplish your own goals.

The well-developed Aquarius Midheaven can be a skilled manager. The ability to remain objective when others are not can get you over the bumps in life's path and can allow work to flow more smoothly and easily. Such an individual can help others to eliminate energy drains that have decreased individual effectiveness, and to focus on creative processes.

The unconscious intuitive skill that is brought to bear is the steady application of discriminating awareness (found in the movement from a water sign to a fire sign). The Aquarius Midheaven needs to be clear enough to receive intuitive signals from the unconscious about the situation. If the mind is too busy with worry or frustration, then intuition cannot come into play. When there is clarity, this individual can discriminate among the choices available, and can consistently identify paths of less resistance—intuitively. As this information enters consciousness, a bit of practical testing will show how to use the information effectively.

The Pure Energy of Aquarius on the Midheaven
The second thinking style of the Aquarius Midheaven lies in the application of the energy of the pure fixed air sign. In Buddhist psychology, the resting in one

element reflects the nature of that element, and places it in a container of wisdom. This is a wisdom much larger than the intellect of Aquarius. It is the wisdom of all-encompassing space. The Aquarius Midheaven can, in ideal moments, achieve the breadth and depth of wisdom of the saints in communion with God, or the direct contact with Universal Mind, or the sudden knowledge of realizations small and large. When the world is seen to be all of a piece—as Unity—then there is no limit to what can be accomplished.

However, this space is not without its perils. The neurotic response to the perception of such groundlessness is painful. Traditionally called *agoraphobia,* or fear of the marketplace or open space, this fear effectively shuts off any message coming into the individual awareness. Only personal security seems worth pursuing in such a moment.

The adjustment needed to steer away from this fear lies in the intuition of Leo, the sign on the Nadir. Leo offers inspiration that comes from the deepest well of your being. It is supported by idealism of the heart, an excellent supplement to the intellectual idealism of Aquarius. It promises the freedom of the spirit that is necessary if the all-encompassing quality of knowledge is to be appreciated. It promises that you don't need to focus on your individual center in order to maintain it. The nobility and dignity of leadership are based on this upwelling of inner courage and faith.

Aquarius/Pisces Cusp

The third thinking style associated with Aquarius is reflected in the transition from Aquarius to Pisces, or fixed air to mutable water. In alchemy the movement from air to water takes you from intellectual objectivity into the murky waters of the unconscious, where you feel you will dissolve. The need to maintain a space for yourself by creating rigid boundaries may keep you insulated from the larger world of feeling because you live in fear of being suffocated by all that is outside the self. This can express as claustrophobia, or fear of being closed in by the outside world. It at first appears to be the opposite of agoraphobia (fear of being in too large a space), but it is actually part of the continuum of how you respond to pressures from the outer world or from within the self. In this neurotic style you so fear being smothered that you erect boundaries large enough to keep you safe, but they keep things out that may be valuable to you as well.

One path to managing this kind of fear is to become precise in your analysis. On the opposite side of the chart—the Nadir—Leo is changing to Virgo, the sign of precise, detailed, scientific thinking. Allow the inner voice to speak to you in as precise terms as possible. If you are open to this voice, you get all the details you need from the limitless well of information stored within your mind. You can then evaluate the intuitive information by applying intellect. You can research the material world for facts to support the inner voice. By doing the intellectual work, you deal with the world in an orderly fashion, born out of your unconscious capacity to serve.

Summary

In the positive expression of the Aquarius Midheaven, *knowing* becomes a felt sense of awareness that connects the instinctual level of mind with conscious expression in the world. The normally intellectual Aquarius Midheaven comes to know that he or she can depend on the gut feelings that arise. For Aquarius, as well as other air signs, meditation on one object or on the breath can facilitate the expansion of awareness, allowing intuition to come through. Because the inner source is grounded in faith and fearless determination, conscious focusing on these qualities can help them into expression.

Conscious Choice

If, on the other hand, ego-consciousness allows for new input, even a traumatic event is met with a more flexible attitude. There is room for the traumatic information to exist in consciousness so that the individual can work through it. There is a willingness to seek help—to admit that you don't know everything about how to solve this problem. There is a continual sense of growing in knowledge instead of the rigid sense of knowing everything.

Conscious action is a response to the external world based on awareness of what is occurring, rather than reaction based on responses to events in the past. Reaction is an instinctual response, while conscious action is based on a framework of thought. The ideal is to be a spiritual force in the world, using personal knowledge and experience effectively in each life situation that arises.

Creative Expression

Aquarius is a fixed sign. This means that the intellect can tend to become rigid, incapable of breaking out of familiar thought patterns. The individual then tends to think only of self and loses any sense of vision of a larger reality. Meditation can provide a means of opening the mind to larger possibilities. The Aquarius Midheaven knows it can grasp larger ideas, and generally welcomes the fresh air of insight. As the mind develops the flexibility to engage with new ideas, the resulting spaciousness provides the means for creative process.

This spacious mind can be experienced without meditation, of course. It is frequently found that some means of focusing the mind is helpful, if not to inspire creative ideas, then to determine the means to implement them in the material world. Each individual perceives the mental space differently. Some may see a blank page upon which to write. Others may feel the room to move physically. Profound silence may signal the emergence of a different voice. The Aquarius Midheaven could respond by rejecting the thought that any gap could exist, or may view the emptiness as a receptacle to be filled joyously and creatively.

Spiritual Awareness

On the surface, awareness comes from contact with the world and subsequent thought. For the Aquarius Midheaven, however, the most profound awareness depends on a development of mind. First the intellect is trained through education, through reading, and through interaction with others. At some point the intuitive mechanism arises, and it, too, is cultivated. When these two are joined in a flexible mind, whatever enters awareness can be evaluated from several perspectives, and judgment can be withheld until the intellect has engaged fully. This is an ideal spiritual awareness that must be developed over time.

Mary Shelley

Mary Shelley changed the face of fiction with her novel *Frankenstein* (chart 43). In addition, she in many ways exemplified the free spirit that young people continue to admire today. She eloped with Percy while he was still married to Harriet Westbrook Shelley, and they spent time with Byron in Italy. Two years later she had a dream that was to become her best-known novel. At the time there was some controversy over the intent of the novel—whether it attacked romantic philosophy, or romantic science—but today it seems evident that the content of her disturbing dream struck a chord with her contemporaries and has continued to do so to this day.

Of her work, Mary Shelley said, "Invention, it must be humbly admitted, does not exist in creating out of void, but out of chaos; the materials must, in the

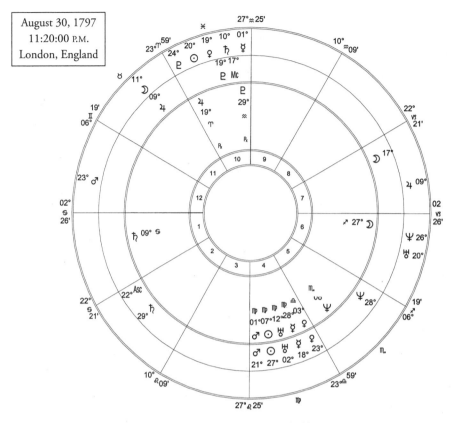

Chart 43. Mary Shelley

first place be afforded; it can give form to dark, shapeless substances, but cannot bring into being the substance itself" (Miller, p. 59). The creative inspiration for *Frankenstein* arose from the Leo fire of the IC in her birth chart.

At the time of publication solar arc Midheaven squared the North Node (indicative of the author-publisher relationship) and solar arc Sun formed a quincunx to the Midheaven (showing success). Solar arc Neptune squared the Midheaven (devotion to an objective) during the period when the work was being written, along with solar arc Saturn quincunx the Midheaven (slow development).

Perhaps the more interesting aspects occurred at the time of the dream, and indicate the state of her mind at the time. I have included the entire list:

Solar Arc Planet Aspect to Natal Planet	Delineation
Uranus conjunct Venus	*strong emotional tension*
Pluto square North Node	karmic destiny
Jupiter opposition Neptune	rich emotional expression
Saturn sextile Mercury	depth of thought
Mars quincunx Jupiter (past)	power to concentrate
Sun conjunct Mercury	*active mind, change of direction*
Sun square Moon	*conscious/unconscious contrast*
Sun quincunx Midheaven	*awareness of one's objective*
Mercury sextile South Node	opportunity for influence by others
Mercury trine North Node	desire to exchange ideas with others
Neptune square Midheaven	*devotion to strange goals*
Neptune quincunx Moon	subconscious activity
Neptune sextile Mercury	imagination
Ascendant into Second House	movement into the productive phase of life

The large amount of activity accounts for the drama of Mary Shelley's life in general, and to some extent for the dream filled with horror. The Midheaven-IC aspects in italics focus on the developing self-awareness that allowed her to write her story. The other aspects indicate the ambiance surrounding her at the time and the psychic pressure that produced the inspiring dream.

It is interesting to note that while we may not treat dream life very seriously, in this and other cases it was dream material that changed the course of events for individuals and for nations. Dreams provide more than material for good stories. In this case a dream provided Mary Shelley with a novel that has never been out of print, and that has been a focal point of twentieth-century horror stories. By revealing her frightening dream, Mary Shelley has contributed to our greater awareness of the contents of the unconscious—which was the source of the story in the first place.

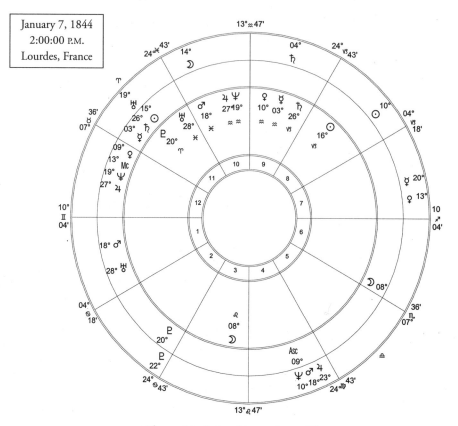

Chart 44. Saint Bernadette Chart #1

Saint Bernadette

Saint Bernadette claimed to have had eighteen visitations from the Virgin Mary (chart 44).[1] Bernadette suffered from extensive publicity, and eventually withdrew to a convent, where she spent the rest of her life. The spot where she had the visions has become a shrine, visited by thousands of people seeking to be healed by the healing powers of the water in the spring.

At the time of her visions, Bernadette's solar arc Midheaven formed a semi-sextile to Uranus (ruler of the Midheaven) and solar arc Uranus formed a sextile to the Midheaven. In the previous year her solar arc Sun entered Aquarius. The highly unusual nature of her visions is reflected in aspects both to and from the Midheaven, indicating that she was both fully self-aware and open to the opportunity of the visions. Her decision to enter the convent is reflected in transiting Uranus and Pluto in her twelfth house.

---

1. Rodden, p. 288.

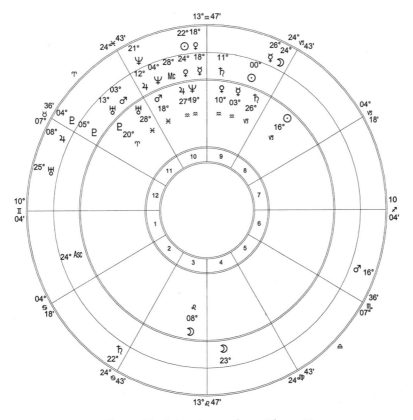

Chart 45. Saint Bernadette Chart #2

Evidence seems to support the truth of her stories. She was canonized in 1933 after passing the Church's tests. Many people would say they were indeed healed when the visited Lourdes. At the time of her canonization (chart 45), the solar arc chart formed a square to the birth chart. Transiting Uranus, ruler of her Midheaven, sextiled Neptune in the tenth house, and transiting Neptune was quincunx Venus in Aquarius. Through no apparent effort on her part, Bernadette has found a place of adoration in the hearts of millions of believers.

Neil Armstrong

There is a discrepancy in the quoted birth place for Neil Armstrong (chart 46).[2] Many sources mention Wapakoneta, Ohio. In *AstroDatabank*, Lois Rodden

2. www.astronaut.org/astronauts/armstrong.htm.

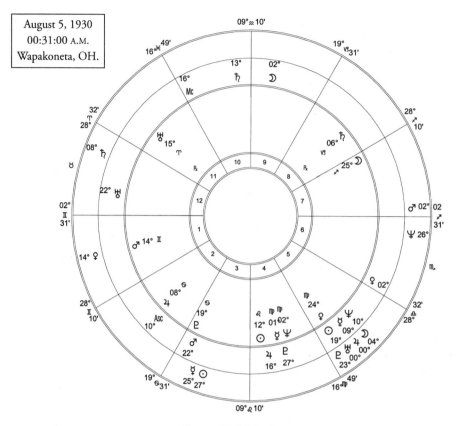

Chart 46. Neil Armstrong

mentions Washington, Ohio. The difference between the two locations is less than one degree of longitude and just over one degree of latitude.

Neil Armstrong exemplifies the Aquarius Midheaven and its ruler, Uranus. His career as a naval aviator and astronaut goes to the essence of the transition from earth to air. His intellect served him well in these careers, and later as a professor of aeronautical engineering. In 1969 he became the first human to set foot on the Moon, a landmark moment in history.

In the birth chart the Sun opposes the Midheaven, indicating an awareness of the balance between his individuality and his ego. The quincunx from Jupiter suggests that he may have had to adjust his expansiveness to suit the rigors of his training programs. The Mars trine reflects his dynamic energy that he threw into his work.

At the moment he stepped onto the surface of the Moon, solar arc Mercury (ruler of the Ascendant) applied to trine the Midheaven. He experienced a moment of perfect consistency between his physical being and his mind. This did not occur without stress. He had solar arc Ascendant sesqui-square the Moon and solar arc Uranus (ruler of the Midheaven) semi-square Jupiter. Transiting aspects included Mars opposite the Ascendant, Saturn square the Midheaven, and Pluto sesqui-square the Midheaven. The closely structured space flight, intense experience of landing on the Moon, and the exhilaration of walking on its surface are all shown in these aspects.

Other Aquarius Midheavens

Christa McAuliffe, September 2, 1948, 10:13 P.M., Boston, Massachusetts

Herbert Hoover, August 10, 1874, 11:12 P.M., West Branch, Iowa

Arthur Conan Doyle, May 22, 1859, 4:55 A.M., Edinburgh, Scotland

Leonard Nimoy, March 26, 1931, 8:30 A.M., Boston, Massachusetts

Martin Luther King Jr., January 15, 1929, 1:00 P.M., Atlanta, Georgia

Phyllis Diller, July 17, 1917, 1:00 A.M., Lima, Ohio

Julia Child, August 15, 1912, 11:30 P.M., Pasadena, California

Scott Carpenter, May 1, 1925, 6:45 A.M., Boulder, Colorado

Shelley Winters, August 18, 1922, 12:05 A.M., St. Louis, Missouri

14

PISCES MIDHEAVEN

When Pisces is at the Midheaven in the Northern Hemisphere, the angle between the Ascendant and Midheaven is over 90 degrees. At the Ascendant the smallest possible angle is very close to 90 degrees, while at 40 degrees the angle can be as much as 115 degrees and at 55 degrees of latitude as much as 130 degrees. The Pisces Midheaven person will tend to be responsive to outside influences. This is consistent with what we know about Pisces, a sign that is impressionable and sensitive. Of course, if many planets fall in the Eastern Hemisphere, this tendency will be balanced with self-assertive attitudes, creating a more assertive personality.

Wait-and-See Attitude

Pisces Midheavens can sit back and watch what is happening around them, waiting to see what develops. They have an internal clock that dictates their own speed, so they do not depend on traditional time frames. They sense the speed at which a project may unfold, as well as the process of that unfolding, so they know when they can afford to wait. It is odd to consider this "instinct" as a trait of the Midheaven because ego-consciousness is not generally thought to be instinctual; the key is that Pisces Midheavens know how time functions as a variable, not as a constant.

Instability
Pisces Midheavens demonstrate instability from time to time, perhaps as a result of this unusual relationship to time. Again, Pisces Midheavens know what is happening, where Pisces Sun or Moon might feel but not understand the energy of the moment. Also, Pisces is impressionable on the psychic level. When one is channeling or receiving telepathically or whatever, the normal flow of activities is interrupted, thus creating the impression of instability. Self-awareness develops for the Pisces Midheaven through awareness of this movement within consciousness.

Impressionability
The way in which Pisces Midheavens receive psychic information will determine what they know about themselves to a large extent. Some will know themselves through feelings, some through intuitive insights, some through channeling or transmission. Some will not recognize any of these capabilities but will say they are very sympathetic and compassionate toward others. Some will be aware in such a natural way that they cannot say how the process works.

As ego-consciousness develops, Pisces Midheavens shift from less controlled mediumship into greater compassionate awareness. Clairvoyance becomes spiritual perception, clairaudience becomes inspiration, instinct develops into intellect, selfishness transmutes to selflessness, etc. Pisces Midheavens know they are psychically sensitive; what they do with it is related to personal will and use of power.

Desire for Simplicity
Pisces Midheavens like to maintain simplicity in their lives. They know that psychic energies can complicate situations and they need maneuvering room. Albert Einstein, a Pisces Midheaven, sought to reduce the complexities of the universe into one simple equation. One way in which mutable signs simplify things is to see them as continua of basic energies. Pisces Midheavens understand polarities in this way. For example, Pisces may experience the pain of another person. Rather than think of it as a separate, real, permanent thing, they think of it as part of the continuum of joy. This makes it easier to help the individual through the pain and toward greater happiness. The pain is not ignored, but neither is it solidified.

Easy Life with Occasional Pleasures
Ebertin (p. 69) mentions that the Pisces Midheaven indicates a striving for a simple and easy life. This characteristic is difficult to understand when one examines

the list of Pisces Midheavens, including Marie Curie, Theodore Roosevelt, Kaiser Wilhelm, and even Jesse James. These people had complicated lives. Yet in each case one can see an area in which the individual cut through a lot of issues to arrive at simple strategies and tactics, simplified understanding of the world, and basic approaches to situations.

Each Pisces Midheaven knows the inner, personal requirements for a simple life and basic pleasures. Thus, what appears to me to be intensely complicated and unpleasant may appeal to some internal model for the Pisces Midheaven, a model that is elegant yet complete.

Philosophical Interests

Because the path of development involves awareness of polarities of all kinds, Pisces Midheavens sometimes develop an interest in philosophy. They may study various systems that have application in their personal lives, gleaning value from each theory and adapting it to their own uses. Where Libra walks the middle path, Pisces Midheavens will often step off the path to experience the extremes of positive and negative energy. For Pisces the goal is to learn about polarity; for Libra the goal is to achieve balance. The learning tasks are different. Pisces needs patience to follow through with the whole experience, while Libra may only need a taste to know they are off center. Once the negative has been experienced, then Pisces Midheavens know how they feel about it and can go on to higher, more positive outlets for their creativity.

Desire for Seclusion

All very sensitive people long for time alone in which to rest and recover their sense of harmony. Pisces Midheavens are quite conscious of their own needs. They plan their lives to include the time-outs, knowing that they will be refreshed and inspired. Time spent in seclusion results in clarification of misunderstandings of all kinds. Difficult interactions can be placed against a background of spiritual well-being, and compassion can take the place of irritation. Pisces Midheavens can talk a good line about their beliefs; without time in seclusion they may not be able to walk the path they profess to see so clearly.

Resistance

Resistance lies between what one has and what one wishes to have. Pisces Midheavens know that they can have higher spiritual perception, more compassion for others, and deeper intellect. They must be willing to let go of earlier developmental achievements in order to progress further. For example, a Pisces Midheaven has developed a schedule that includes one day a week in seclusion at home. This time is used to recharge and to think through events of the previous six days. The individual becomes attached to this schedule and even demands the day off.

Events may arise in which other family members or friends are injured or seriously ill. If the recharging during seclusion has worked, then the day off can be used to visit the people who need help because a reserve of energy exists. The resting day can be postponed in service of friends and family. It has prepared Pisces to handle a crisis, but is not a life requirement. Pisces Midheavens then move through their resistance to upsets in the schedule, realizing the higher value of preparation for service.

Capacity to Respond

Pisces Midheavens know, then, that they can respond in crisis situations. They can also respond to the daily events in their children's lives, the development of relationships, or whatever situations arise. The sensitivity that may have begun as a problem in childhood has developed into a refined method for understanding the needs of people around them. They know they can get the feel for situations quickly and respond to the flow of psychic energy properly. Thus the capacity to respond is dependent on the level of self-awareness the Pisces Midheaven has achieved. Knowing instinctively develops into intellect and knowing clairvoyantly develops into spiritual perception. At the same time acquiring more for the self can develop into renunciation of personal needs in favor of service to others. Then the capacity to respond is fuller and richer.

Sanity and Neurosis

The three thinking styles associated with Pisces at the Midheaven include the following astrological correspondences:

1. The cusp of Aquarius and Pisces, or the movement from fixed air to mutable water.

2. The pure energy of the mutable water sign itself.

3. The cusp of Pisces and Aries, or the movement from mutable water to cardinal fire.

These three relationships describe both the neurotic potential of Pisces on the Midheaven and the sanity to be found there.

Aquarius/Pisces Cusp

Pisces swings between opposites that are bridging the gap between personality drives and selfless service. Therefore the neuroses which arise can be intensely painful and difficult. The first area of neurosis involves air changing to water. For the resistant Pisces Midheaven there can be intense anger when one is required to give up what one has. There is an immediate focus on the object of the anger that excludes other realities. With no apparent care for the results, Pisces can undercut the opponent with razor-sharp memory of past difficulties and insults, along with sarcastic retorts that are designed to harm.

This anger, in touch with memory and quick as it is, is not so separate from the clarity that expresses sanity. Pisces Midheavens will experience the angry outburst as totally separate from their normal intellectual clarity. The fact is that clarity is based on the very skills that make the anger so exquisite. The difference is that clarity has a breadth of vision that places each experience in a larger picture. Calm water reflects the sky perfectly; totally calm water can also allow us to see into the depths as though the water was not there. For Pisces Midheavens, clarity has both qualities. They can cultivate the clarity while accepting the anger as part of their own process, thereby owning both sides of this powerful energy.

The Pure Energy of Pisces

The second thinking style of Pisces involves the energy of the pure mutable water sign. This neurosis is based on staying with the energy of Pisces and relates to the spaciousness or lack of same. The neurotic response is one of indifference toward others. This indifference is a result of a neurotic process of freezing one's own pain. If the pain is frozen, we think, it can be managed. It does not move around or grow. We learn through experience that this is only a stop-gap measure—sooner or later we all must look our own suffering.

Another facet of this neurosis is the fear of death or emptiness. Imagine what it would be like to not have the pain that was frozen and stored. There would be empty space! If there is space, then there is an awareness of death as well. This is far more frightening than the concept of freezing pain in order to store it.

In order to experience the sanity of Pisces, one requires spaciousness. Using pain as an example, if there is space in which the pain can move, it will dissipate.

One experiences the pain but does not own it, does not hold on to it. Then there is room for another feeling, and another. Pisces Midheavens know that they have the capacity not only for their own feelings, but for the feelings of others. If there is a stuck area, a frozen area, one not only is not dealing with personal pain, one is unable to face that same kind of pain in another individual. The result is denial of the other person's reality. The intelligence of space is to make Pisces aware of such fixed psychic processes and to dissolve them.

Pisces/Aries Cusp

The third thinking style of Pisces is concerned with the transition from Pisces to Aries, or mutable water to cardinal fire. Whereas Pisces Midheavens know that they have finely developed discriminative power, they occasionally will find themselves stuck in a cycle of acquisitiveness in which there is not letting go, only getting more. This process allows for no appreciation, as the foremost task is to find a place to put the new idea, the new object. Since nothing has been moved out, there is no place to put anything, and this generates feelings of claustrophobia. Thus the urge to have everything we desire becomes clotted and closed in.

Openness in terms of this neurosis involves true compassion. We convert the passion to acquire things into compassion for others. Pisces Midheavens know the value of clarity when they are listening to the flow of other people's thoughts and feelings. One cannot be stuck in one's own feelings and expect to find that flow. Think of the artificial flower. It captures the appearance of the real flower, but never wilts. Once beautiful artificial flowers occupy the vase in which real flowers could be placed, one cannot have real flowers there. To have real flowers, one must accept them for what they are, throwing them out when their beauty has faded. To have real feelings, one must feel them and let them go when the feelings have faded. One can trust that another feeling will come along.

This natural flow of feelings and ideas finds its place in the metaphor of spring. The transition from Pisces to Aries in the tropical zodiac is the vernal equinox. This is the time when nature moves from the dormant period of winter into the new growth made possible by the Sun's movement into northern latitudes. The passage into spring does not demand the removal of all life and a total renewal. It does indicate a time when the full expression of the previous year, encapsulated within the seed, bursts forth from the earth to renew the life cycle.

Whereas Aries is focused on the moment the new sprout peeks out from the ground, Pisces is remembering all that went into the development of that seed. The Aries Midheaven may find it easy to let go of the old and strike out in a new direction. The Pisces Midheaven must learn the letting go process.

Creativity

Pisces Midheavens are at their most creative when they engage in compassionate service. The flow of their energy allows them to perform such works freely and easily, taking care of themselves in the process. Neptune as ruler of Pisces focuses the devotion that Pisces can mobilize in service to others. Jupiter, the traditional ruler, emphasizes the wisdom and love required. Expansive acquisition is converted into extensive service. Esoterically Pisces Midheavens mobilize the will and power of Pluto to maintain their own energy and to fuel their creative processes. According to Alice Bailey, all of this is a result of the psychic opening that occurs as Pisces enters the path (Bailey, p. 125).

Conscious Choice

Free will for Pisces Midheavens lies in the determination to shift from an ego-centric view of reality to a sympathetic relationship with others. This change is facilitated by growing psychic sensitivity. An interesting facet of the shift toward selflessness is the fact that as one gives, one receives in like measure. Thus one's stores do not become depleted, but rather are freshened in the process. Pisces Midheavens know how to mobilize the will and they recognize the significance of personal power; directing that power into service is a freeing process leading to enlightenment.

Spiritual Growth

Self-realization comes through experience. In every area there is a shift from desire for personal satisfaction and personal understanding toward attention to the needs of others. All spiritual growth depends on developing the intellect to discriminate among choices. At some point Pisces Midheavens realize that they used to have "feelings" about the people and events around them, and now they have a deeper perception and understanding of their relationship to others. A gradual detachment from the physical realm leads to identification with spirit and a profound understanding of death as part of life's cyclical process.

Sally Ride

On June 18, 1983, Sally Ride became the first American woman to reach outer space (chart 47). A physically and intellectually strong woman, she had excelled as a tennis player and as a student. Her graduate work was in physics, including x-ray astronomy. Her mechanical education and skills, as well as her demonstrated facility for teamwork, were key factors in her acceptance into the astronaut program.

In the planning for the 1983 flight, Sally helped to develop a mechanical arm that would be used to deploy a test satellite. In 1984 she solved mechanical problems that lead to the successful launch of an earth radiation satellite. Later in her career she served as a planner for the future of NASA, and was part of the presidential commission to study the explosion of the tenth flight of Challenger.

At the time of the 1983 flight, Sally had a solar of just over 30 degrees and solar arc Uranus was past the semi-square to the Midheaven (both indicating that the hard work and stress was in the past). Solar arc Jupiter formed a semi-square to the Midheaven (reflecting both the stress of the space flight and the attainment of success). (The solar arc Ascendant squared Mercury, ruler of the fourth house (indicating a change of residence!). Solar arc Neptune (ruler of the Midheaven) trined Venus (the joy of the event and the high ideals being put into play), and squared Pluto (self-knowledge, the capacity to pursue unusual work, and a powerful vision of her future). By transit Mars squared the Midheaven, reflecting ego-conscious action, based on readiness, and the attainment of her goals).

Her own assessment of the first flight into space is a definitive statement about her connection to her life and work: "The thing that I'll remember most about the flight is that it was fun. In fact, I'm sure that it was the most fun that I will ever have in my life" (Hurwitz, p. 99). Like many reported peak experiences, this one involved many years of education, training, and teamwork. Yet all that effort is summed up in the statement "It was fun."

Chief Crazy Horse

Although there is some controversy about the birth date and time for Crazy Horse, I have included this brief example because it reflects the compelling quality of Pisces at the Midheaven (chart 48). Shy as a child, he didn't acquire his

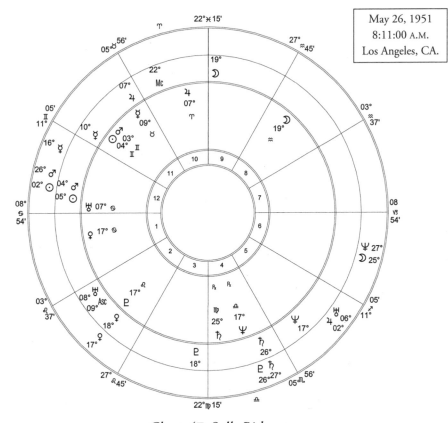

Chart 47. Sally Ride

name until after a big battle in 1858, when his father, the original Crazy Horse, gave the name to his son. Crazy Horse was a revered warrior of the Lakota Sioux, a leader of the resistance to the U.S. government's efforts to force settlement of the Pine Ridge reservation. He fought General George Crook in 1875 and also at the Battle of the Little Bighorn in 1876.

At the age of thirteen Crazy Horse went out alone to seek a vision. After many days the vision came: "His horse coming toward him from the lake, holding his head high, moving his legs freely. He was carrying a rider, a man with long brown hair hanging loosely . . . The horse kept changing colors. It seemed to be floating" (Freedman, p. 32–34). He was told never to wear a war bonnet and not to paint his horse or tie up its tail . . . instead sprinkle it with dust, then rub some dust over his own hair and body. Also he was told never to take anything

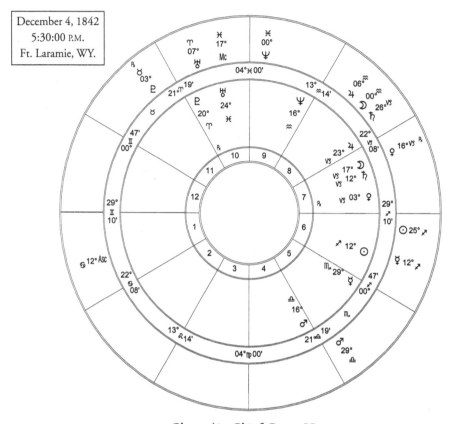

December 4, 1842
5:30:00 P.M.
Ft. Laramie, WY.

Chart 48. Chief Crazy Horse

away from a battle. In this way no arrow or rifle could kill him. Crazy Horse did not tell his father of this vision until he was sixteen years old. His father agreed that it was a powerful vision and urge his son to follow the instructions. After he surrendered at Fort Robinson in May 1877, Crazy Horse was killed by a knife wound in the back.

In the birth chart the Midheaven was semi-square Pluto. At the time of his vision, solar arc Pluto formed a sextile to the Midheaven (an opportunity to recognize his mission in life). Solar arc Neptune, ruler of the Midheaven, moved from Aquarius into Pisces (inclining him to psychic or mystical influence). Solar arc Mars was semi-sextile Mercury, ruler of the IC and the Ascendant (the achievement of a goal through determination). Solar arc Mercury conjuncted the Sun (moving toward a new objective). Solar arc Venus was semi-sextile Neptune indicating he could be easily influenced and also indicating his high ideals at the time.

Jesse Ventura

Television wrestler or governor of Minnesota? If you had read Jesse Ventura's chart for him fifteen years ago, it would have been a very tough call. What career would you have recommended to him (chart 49)?[1]

Looking at the Midheaven in the natal chart, we find the angle between Ascendant and Midheaven is 117 degrees. Generally this indicates that Jesse tends to respond to other people, and can certainly make the effort to please his constituents. He has the Sun and five planets on the eastern half of the chart, indicating a tendency to assert his own style. Between these two factors, and considering Mars and Uranus in the first house, we can guess that he will have a style all his own, and that he will be able to pour energy into whatever he does.

His career in the navy suits the Pisces Midheaven. The wrestling career is a natural growth into Aries in the tenth house. For many people the second (or even third) sign in the tenth house indicates a subsequent career. With Mars in the first House, wrestling used Jesse's abundant energy and put him in the limelight.

Looking at Jesse's chart for 1985, another career change could be predicted. Solar arc Midheaven sesqui-square Pluto is a past aspect, indicating that the dynamic tension of the career may be waning. Solar arc Midheaven is quincunx Venus, suggesting that any adjustment must come from him—from his own self-awareness. Solar arc Ascendant trine the Midheaven indicates that the conditions are right for change to occur. With Neptune sextiling the birth Midheaven by transit and Uranus sextile natal Neptune, more television or acting is an obvious choice. Numerous other aspects define and refine the nature of the changes that are possible. Within two to three years, solar arc Saturn trined the Midheaven and solar arc Midheaven squared Mars. At that time Jesse faced conditions that forced him to give up wrestling—some said it was due to exposure to Agent Orange, others said he had serious rib injuries. He developed a successful career as color commentator for wrestling and starred in *Predator*. A line from this movie became the title of Jesse's book, published in 1999, *I Ain't Got Time to Bleed*, published after his successful bid for the governor's office in Minnesota.

By 1991 the chart indicates another major change that could affect career. Solar arc Uranus conjuncted natal Pluto and solar arc Pluto conjuncted natal

1. www.geocities.com/Colosseum.3025/Ventura.htm.

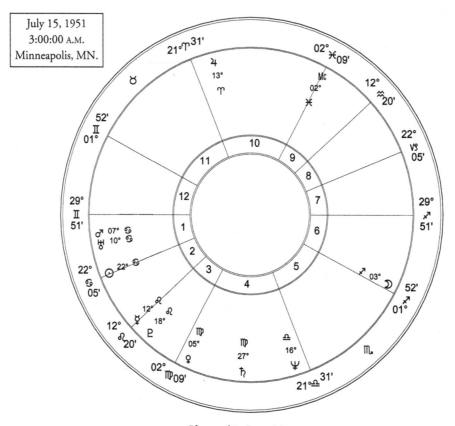

July 15, 1951
3:00:00 A.M.
Minneapolis, MN.

Chart 49. Jesse Ventura

Saturn. Solar arc Mars was sextile Neptune—rulers of both tenth-house signs reflected the opportunity for change. Venus opposed Jupiter and the Sun moved into Virgo by solar arc in February or 1991. Looking at the Midheaven, solar arc Midheaven squared Uranus. This single aspect provided a major impulse for change, with Jesse engineering the change, based on his intuitive self-awareness. Transiting Uranus opposed its birthplace, strengthening the Midheaven aspect and providing awareness of what the public was thinking.

Jesse Ventura's chart demonstrates that a focus on the Midheaven and its aspects, both in the birth chart and by progression and transit, can reflect both the mood and the events concerning career and career change. The more a client can gain self-awareness, the better he or she is able to manage career decisions.

Other Pisces Midheavens

J. S. Bach, March 31, 1685, 9:38 A.M., Eisenbach, Germany

Peter Fonda, February 23, 1939, 12:09 P.M., Manhattan, New York

Noel Tyl, December 31, 1936, 3:57 P.M., West Chester, Pennsylvania

Mary Decker, August 4, 1958, 2:59 A.M., Deptford, New Jersey

Ronald Reagan, February 6, 1911, 2:00 P.M., Tampico, Illinois

Fidel Castro, August 13, 1927, 2:00 A.M., Colonia Biran, Cuba (some sources say 1926)

Marcia Moore, May 22, 1928, 9:10 A.M., Cambridge, Massachusetts

Farrah Fawcett, February 2, 1947, 3:10 P.M., Corpus Christi, Texas

Carry Nation, November 25, 1846, 7:30 P.M., Garrard Co., Kentucky

Marie Curie, November 7, 1867, 8:45 P.M., Warsaw, Poland

15

NATAL ASPECTS AND TRANSITS TO THE MIDHEAVEN

In the natal chart the time of day determines the Midheaven. If we think of the Midheaven as a fixed point in the southern sky, the zodiac transits clockwise across that point at the rate of one degree every four minutes. If we think of the Midheaven as a moving point, it transits forward through the zodiac (counterclockwise) at the same rate. Therefore the Midheaven applies to and separates from aspects to all the planets and is mutually applying or separating to retrograde planets. The transiting Midheaven is not often used in natal astrology, but diurnal motion becomes very significant in such applications as business and gambling, to name only two.

In terms of direction and progression the Midheaven moves at the same speed as the Sun when it is calculated according to solar arc. In solar arc directions every object moves at the same speed. In secondary progressions each planet moves at the rate of a day for a year. The Midheaven moves at the speed of the Sun, and the Ascendant is calculated from the progressed Midheaven at the new location of the individual. In progressed charts the Moon, Mercury, Venus, and the Ascendant may be moving faster than the Midheaven.

Natal Aspects Involving the Midheaven

The zodiacal sign of the Midheaven is the first consideration. We get a benchmark understanding of the nature of an individual's self-awareness from the degree at the Midheaven The previous chapters have elaborated the meaning of the Midheaven in each of the signs. To expand this understanding we integrate the Midheaven with the rest of the chart through aspects to the planets. The following section focuses closely on the nature of ego-consciousness as defined in previous chapters, and draws heavily on the work of Reinhold Ebertin, *The Combination of Stellar Influences*. This book is still the best summary of midpoints as well as aspects between planets.

Midheaven to Sun

Your individuality and self-awareness have a natural connection. While some people struggle to find out who they are, you are busy deciding how to make the most of what you know about yourself. If there is no aspect between the Sun and Midheaven in your birth chart, you experience periods of time when you actively question your inner motives. Directions and transits involving the Midheaven give all of us the opportunity to learn about ourselves, revealing the interaction between individuality and self-awareness in refreshing ways.

Midheaven to Moon

Self awareness and your soul life are integrally connected. You often seem to get messages from your inner self that guide your steps spiritually. Your deep source of values pushes you to understand yourself and your life direction more fully. You seek a flexible life plan that includes a nurturing role of some kind, based on what you have learned about yourself. You have broad interests that help to ground your personal values. The Moon serves as a conduit for unconscious material to arise. The Midheaven then indicates your method of engaging the unconscious flow and using it to develop greater self-awareness. You discover your spirituality indirectly and integrate it through more concrete means. When there is no aspect between the Moon and Midheaven, look to the Sun first, and then the other planets as they relate to the Midheaven. The ruler of the IC may be the most direct contact with your inner voice.

Midheaven to Mercury

Your communication style is a significant factor in how you gain self-awareness. It is important for you to train your mind so that you have two-way flow of information with your inner being, as well as with the outer world. You are able to examine and modify your mental processes directly. The changeable quality of Mercury means that you have to be able to recognize yourself in many forms. Meditation or other mind training is very important. This combination makes it possible for you to understand many sides of a situation, and to communicate the values needed to resolve differences. When there is no aspect between Mercury and the Midheaven, communication as a self-awareness tool must be consciously trained, and is reflected in the aspects Mercury makes to other planets.

Midheaven to Venus

Traditional astrology calls Venus the "social planet," interested in beauty and balance. Esoteric astrology gives Venus the capacity for concrete knowledge—that is, the absorption of factual material. Venus-Midheaven aspects indicate that the social venue is key to the understanding of inner motivations. You may be more at home examining the situations other people get themselves into than looking deep within yourself. If you can become a cooperative partner with your inner self, you will find no stronger ally in your path toward self-awareness. A strong Venus Midheaven connection will allow you to manifest your sense of balance in the material world in some way. If there is no aspect between Venus and the Midheaven, the social milieu is not the best way for you to seek self-understanding. Love may be expressed in less conscious, and certainly less conspicuous ways, and it may have an archetypal, primitive quality that you never fully understand.

Midheaven to Mars

Mars in aspect with the Midheaven brings tremendous energy to your personal journey. You are always seeking something new to shed light on the inner side of your life, and you avidly pursue whatever new technique you discover. Some people record their dreams—you press yourself to capture all the nuances of detail, and may have a shelf full of journals. Some people seek new experiences—you make them happen. At the same time you use the body of experience well as a manager and as a determined producer. Ego-conscious action is a valuable commodity—so many people spend their lives acting out unconscious drives without much thought. With age comes greater control of your psychic energy. If there is no Midheaven-Mars aspect, you will find that your energy has a mind of its own, and you may need to actively "work out," both physically and mentally.

Midheaven to Jupiter

Midheaven/Jupiter aspects are some of the most fortunate combinations in the chart. You have the potential for success because you are consciously aware of your higher aims and aspirations. You have a general optimism that is hard to dampen, and you find many things easy. When ideas emerge from the less conscious part of you, you are able to mobilize them into allies. You cheerfully accept your dreams and your inner voice and work with them. For you this communication flows easily most of the time. If there is no Midheaven-Jupiter aspect, your relationship to your spiritual being is somewhat less conscious, but no less profound. You may experience epic dreams, and you may see visions, but you will not be able to do this on demand.

Midheaven to Saturn

Aspects between Saturn and the Midheaven relate the structure of the exterior world to the interior structure. If ego-consciousness is flexible, then the working relationship between interior and exterior reflects adaptability and openness to one's world. If, on the other hand, the ego complex is rigid, the already cautious approach to change becomes almost inert. The nature may become overly self-critical, and this deprives the individual of the ability to establish awareness of the exterior world, or distorts it. The result is difficulty in forming and maintaining healthy relationships. To maintain or increase flexibility, cognitive thinking must be practiced. By this I mean you have to employ logical intellectual processes and eschew judgmental processes. For feeling and intuitive types this can be difficult and even painful, yet it most often results in greater flexibility in future dealings with others and with your intrapsychic dialogue as well. If there is no Midheaven-Saturn aspect, less direct means to relating to structure must be found. Using Saturn's aspects to the planets provides a variety of ways to relate to the material world and to structure in social and psychological situations.

Midheaven to Uranus

In my experience the true role of Uranus is to establish equilibrium within a system. The more out of balance you are, the more extreme the effect of a Uranus transit, as something extreme is needed to bring you back into balance. Thus you may experience aspects of the Midheaven and Uranus as sudden changes in your mental state, decisions to change jobs or move, and events that have tremendous impact on your sense of self and well-being. By the same token, these aspects often indicate times when your intuition is at the ready. You find that the inner voice informs you well and you can take appropriate action without delay. When there is no Midheaven-Uranus aspect, equilibrium is not a conscious consideration. Balance is therefore achieved through instinctual adjustment to circumstances, and imbalance is reflected in other planetary aspects.

Midheaven to Neptune

On the plus side Neptune indicates receptivity, empathy, sensitivity, and a contemplative nature. On the minus side we have deception, illusion, imagination taking over for reason, and lack of clarity in general. All of these less constructive qualities lead to a lack of self-awareness, insecurity, and aimlessness in general. When you have a Neptune-Midheaven contact, it is therefore important to cultivate the more creative, constructive side of the energy, employing will. When there is no Midheaven-Neptune aspect, psychic awareness may be perceived in the body. Moods may be viewed as out of one's personal control to a large extent.

Midheaven to Pluto

Pluto reflects the capacity for force in the chart. The will to exert one's power, as well as the unconscious movement of power, is one side of Pluto-Midheaven aspects. Your individual being is shaped by these forces, whether consciously or unconsciously, so self-awareness becomes significant with the aspects.

There is a sense of mission where Pluto and the Midheaven connect. You can either drive ahead, convinced that your way is the right way, or you can consider the uses of power and exert force in thoughtful, meaningful ways. Both reveal your sense of authority, and both also reveal your self-awareness and awareness of the needs of others. By careful use of your Pluto-Midheaven energies, you can attain a greater sense of independence, and you will feel your less constructive urges transform into positive, creative aspirations. The trained mind manages this energy far better than the unconscious mind. When there is no Midheaven-Pluto aspect, your will is reflected in the aspects Pluto makes. You will need to work to be more conscious of how you exercise your will power.

Progressions, Directions, and Transits to the Midheaven

Because the Midheaven is the most prominent point in the chart, aspects by transit, direction, or progression signal profound changes in self-awareness and attitude. They also reflect major social changes, such as change of residence, shifting family relationships, and career moves. Directions and transits to the Midheaven signal change as no other aspect combinations can. Because these aspects reflect intense pressures on the personality, they are indicators of periods when the most profound changes in self-awareness occur. Often we must be challenged by the world around us before we make inner changes. In fact, most changes are the result of the interaction between the inner being and the outer environment.

Solar Arc Midheaven to Planets

When the Midheaven forms aspects to the planets, major shifts in one's approach to life occur, according to the nature of the planet and the aspect that is formed. The Midheaven reflects self-awareness, and it is that awareness that motivates change.

When a planet moves into an aspect with the natal Midheaven, change occurs, but it is the outer world, reflected by the planet, that initiates the impulse to change, and the ego responds. Events may bring publicity and changes in status that we did not invite, and for which we feel relatively unprepared. Such events are times when we are thankful that we have some self-awareness, and also times when we may experience shifts in ego-consciousness that leave us permanently different.

Aspects to the Midheaven are often mirrored in complementary aspects to the IC. The complementary aspect reveals the nature of the psychic pressure that accompanies the outer event. For example, a square to the Midheaven is paralleled by a square to the IC, indicating that the outer event is matched by an equal interior challenge. A trine to the Midheaven indicates a condition in the outer environment that can be manifested if you take action. The complementary sextile to the IC indicates the opportunity to release psychic energy to make that change occur. Psychologists have identified this connection between the outer and inner life and call the mechanism *projection*. An inner urge is projected onto a person or situation in the outer world that reflects similar energy. Such a projection is neither good nor bad—it is how the mind works. Of course, self-awareness allows you to see your projections for what they are with greater flexibility and grace.

Aspects by progression and direction reflect long-term relationships between a planet and the Midheaven. They show where you are in a cycle of energy, and indicate periods when certain kinds of events and feelings are more likely. They set the stage for events by establishing certain psychic conditions. Transits are shorter-term relationships, for the most part, and indicate the timing of events. Thus an aspect by direction may come and go with little apparent effect, only to be triggered by a transit a short time later. Mars and the Moon are powerful triggers, but other planets can fulfill this role as well. Several transits may occur within the time frame of a progressed or directed aspect, signaling a series of related events. Pay attention to the co-aspect to the IC, as outer Midheaven events often trigger deeper memories or the release of new creative energy from the unconscious.

Aspects to the Midheaven involve three general categories:

1. Changes in status—Events around us like the death of a parent have profound impact on how we approach the rest of our lives. The death doesn't happen to us, but it has a major effect. By contrast, a promotion at work may have relatively little effect on the actual work we do, but it changes our status. The divorce of our parents may cause broad changes in our felt sense of status. These events all involve events outside ourselves and affect self-awareness. Events that we choose may also serve to heighten self-awareness. If you take a new job and leave an old one, your relationship to coworkers changes dramatically. If you choose to move away from home, it may feel like your relationship to your parents dies, or at least undergoes big changes. Even if you choose to divorce your spouse, you cannot avoid the changes in your relationship to your children that will inevitably occur. The differences initially involve where the impulse for change is initiated. Once the change has occurred, changes in self-awareness evolve in much the same way.

2. Stresses to the ego—These can involve health changes or may be the result of how we manage events that occur. We experience resistance, as defined in earlier chapters. Movement within the psyche brings change into conscious awareness and we don't always like it.

3. Changes motivated by shifts in ego-consciousness—Once new self-awareness has developed, we often find that further change in our lives is desirable. We are motivated to move to the next level in relationships, work, or spiritual endeavors.

Self-motivated growth and development come from an awareness of personal mission or spiritual path, and generally are accompanied by a feeling of joy and expectation, and therefore less anxiety and stress than changes that are forced upon us, even though major changes are demanded. We are "in the flow" and change feels natural and right.

Because self-motivated changes are the result of deeper self-awareness, aspects to the IC often provide information about the nature of the inner beliefs that are shaping changes in the outer world. For example, a semi-sextile of the progressed Moon to the IC indicates inner growth, based on newly assimilated psychic material. The co-aspect is a quincunx to the Midheaven, suggesting adjustment on the social sphere to reflect the inner growth. Both levels of activity happen in concert with each other, and the co-aspects reflect the nature of the interactive change.

The following section describes the difference between the aspects of each planet to the Midheaven by direction and transit, and aspects of the directed Midheaven to the planets themselves.

Sun to Midheaven

When the Sun aspects the Midheaven, authority is invoked, generally from the outer environment. Forward progress or loss is the result of your level of self-awareness and the clarity of your goals.

When the Midheaven aspects the Sun, you bring self-awareness to the equation, and actively make decisions concerning your use of personal authority in your life.

Moon to Midheaven

The Moon-Midheaven aspect reflects change in the way you assimilate information and how you feel about it. The Moon aspect may bring a karmic relationship to your awareness. It can also focus your attention on emotional issues in your environment.

When the Midheaven aspects the Moon, you actively affect the emotional environment around you in a conscious way. Instead of succumbing to relatively unconscious impulses, you instead endeavor to act from awareness of your own emotions.

Mercury to Midheaven

Mercury-Midheaven aspects involve communication from the outer environment, and your response to it. Resolution of difficulties often happens on Mercury aspects to the Midheaven.

When the Midheaven forms an aspect to Mercury, you will find that you can consciously formulate your thoughts and communicate them to others. You are positioned to resolve conflicts through clear speech or other means of communciation.

Venus to Midheaven

Venus aspects the Midheaven involve social interaction. Projection of unconscious content into the environment stimulates a response from others, and requires a great deal of self-awareness. Ego-consciousness undergoes profound changes when interpersonal contacts are involved.

Midheaven aspect to Venus bring your conscious mind to focus on social interactions. You are able, through self-awareness, to be more creative and more pro-active in social and romantic situations.

Mars to Midheaven

Mars aspects to the Midheaven involve energy and change. Career changes are common. Emerging unconscious material often stimulates anger, due to a lack of information about how to proceed. We get better at handling Mars transits with age, as we have a track record of previous experience to draw upon.

When the Midheaven aspects Mars, you can embody what you have learned from previous Mars transits to the Midheaven. You are able to act independently, but your actions are more informed and more consistent with your true nature.

Jupiter to Midheaven

Jupiter aspects the Midheaven often indicate success and optimism. Directions set the stage for change and following transits of Mars or the Moon bring the changes to fruition. Aspects to the IC indicate areas of the inner life that are benefiting status.

When the Midheaven aspects Jupiter, you are able to make your own luck. You are acting from your own center and can grasp the essentials of any situation and turn it to your own advantage.

Saturn to Midheaven

Saturn aspects to the Midheaven indicate changes in the structure of the outer environment. There can be difficulty or separation as a result. Restructuring of ego-consciousness is inevitable with big changes, and the IC aspect reflects the unconscious component.

Midheaven aspects to Saturn allow you to use your experience and previous hard work to forge a path that suits your interior structure. You are more in control of your life, meeting your responsibilities and acting with authority that is appropriate to each situation.

Uranus to Midheaven

Uranus aspects to the Midheaven indicate self-assertion. Hasty action brings poor results, while attention to the unconscious motivation brings more fortunate change. The impulse to change emerges from the deepest point of personal equilibrium—the intuition.

When the Midheaven aspects Uranus, you are far more aware of your center of equilibrium. From this balanced position you are able to extend your intuitive senses and evaluate possibilities. When you act, it may seem very sudden to others, but you have probably thought long and hard about the alternatives beforehand.

Neptune to Midheaven

Neptune aspects to the Midheaven are accompanied by relative lack of ego-consciousness. There can be an opening to larger mystical and intuitive understanding which is indeed not grounded in personal ego, but rather is indicative of awareness that transcends the present moment, or that comes from a more spiritual center.

Midheaven aspects to Neptune suggest that you can control the glamour in the situation yourself. You are able to project the part of your personality that is most useful to achieving your personal ends. Compassion flows from a place of self-understanding.

Pluto to Midheaven

Pluto aspects to the Midheaven bring power from the outer environment to bear upon the ego. Self-awareness is one resource against coercion from others, and helps to avoid arguments and moderate what may otherwise be drastic change. Still, you will be subjected to forces for change in a big way.

Midheaven aspects to Pluto, on the other hand, place you in a position to use your self-awareness to influence others. You are able to convince others through the force of your argument, and will want to consider your case carefully before you speak. In this way results will be consistent with your true desires.

CONCLUSION

Crazy Horse and Sally Ride share the experience of having powerful visions that guided their lives. Both had to work for what they sought, and both reached the pinnacle of their careers while gaining the respect of their associates. Mary Shelley had a dream that developed into her greatest novel. The theme of vision and imagination runs through the signs, with some examples of misdirected ego as well.

Each sign at the Midheaven offers a fresh possibility for expanding consciousness and for creative action in the world. Each of us is gifted with these principle challenges—to manifest the self-awareness indicated by the Midheaven, and to evoke our creative best, as indicated by the opposite sign. Along the way we all wrestle with the limitations of mind and seek to overcome them. Suleiman The Magnificent rose to power partly through his father's machinations, but he was successful because of his own vision—he knew he was meant to lead. Christine Sizemore was born into a childhood of deprivation and pain, yet has been able to manifest her personality through stubborn determination. All of the individuals mentioned here share the human capacity to learn about themselves and to use their creative talents because of, or in spite of, the circumstances of their lives.

Hitler and Chaplin—two individuals with very similar talents—show us how the mind can take us to the depths or the heights of possibility. Madonna and Mozart shared similar paths to expression with their Gemini Midheavens, and both were successful in their music careers. The differences in their early training and other areas of their lives played out in their personal lives in very different ways.

Coco Chanel and Colette are two women who had successful careers before it was fashionable for women. They show us how clear self-awareness leads to creative expression and success. Carl Jung spent his life developing a model of the psyche that overcame many of the limitations of his predecessors, and that rekindled our interest in the deepest roots of consciousness—he made it acceptable, and even fashionable, to examine the inner reaches of the psyche.

Each of these people had their own limitations. No one is perfect. However, they show us how we can achieve our best while grappling with our perceived limitations. Hopefully, by understanding your own Midheaven better you will be more successful in dealing with the people around you, and happier in the bargain.

BIBLIOGRAPHY

All Music Guide, A Complete Online Database of Recorded Music. Biography of John Lennon written by Stephen Thomas Erlewine, at www.allmusic.com © 2000 AEC One Stop Group, Inc.

AstroDatabank: Software to Create Better Astrologers. Manchester MA: AstroDatabank Co., 1999.

Bailey, Alice. *Esoteric Astrology.* Lucis Publishing, 1951.

Bartlett. *Familiar Quotations.* Boston: Little, Brown, 1980.

Buddhist Wisdom Books: The Diamond Sutra and the Heart Sutra. Translated by Edward Conze. New York: Harper, 1972.

Chaplin, Charles. *My Autobiography.* New York: Simon & Schuster, 1964.

Chogyam, Nyakpa. *Rainbow of Liberated Energy.* Longmead, England: Element Books, 1986.

Ebertin, Reinhold. *The Combination of Stellar Influences.* Aalen, Germany: Ebertin Verlag, 1972.

Ennis, Stephanie Jean (Clement). *Counseling Techniques in Astrology.* Tempe, AZ: American Federation of Astrologers, 1982.

————. *Decanates and Dwads*. Tempe, AZ: American Federation of Astrologers, 1983.

Fleischer, Nat and Sam Andre. *A Pictorial History of BOXING*. London: Hamlyn, 1998.

Freedman, Russell. *The Life and Death of Crazy Horse*. New York: Holiday House, 1996.

Goodman, Michael Harris. *The Last Dalai Lama: A Biography*. Boston: Shambhala, 1986.

Grell, Paul. *Keywords*. Washington, D.C.: American Federation of Astrologers, 1970.

Grolier Multimedia Encyclopedia, 1995 edition, Version 7.0.5

Hitler, Adolf. *Mein Kampf,* quoted from John Bartlett. *Familiar Quotations,* Boston, Little, Brown 1991. [see entry for Bartlett above].

Holmes, Richard. *Shelley: The Pursuit*. New York: E. P. Dutton, 1975.

Hurwitz, Jane and Sue Hurwitz. *Sally Ride: Shooting for the Stars*. New York: Fawcett Columbine, 1989.

Jung, Carl G. *Collected Works*, Vol. 7. Princeton: Princeton University Press.

Kinross, Lord. *The Ottoman Empire: The Rise and Fall of the Turkish Empire*. New York: William Morrow, 1977.

Kramer, Rita. *Maria Moutessori: A Biography.* New York: Putnam, 1976.

Matrix Software. Celebrity AstroSearch Online Worldwide. Celebrity Birth Database. www.astrologysoftware.com Matrix Software, 1999.

McKay-Clements, John. *The Canadian Astrology Collection*. Toronto: Canadian Astrology Press, 1998.

McMichael, George. ed. *Concise Anthology of American Literature*. 2nd edition. New York: Macmillan, 1984.

Miller, Calvin Craig. *Spirit Like a Storm: The Story of Mary Shelley*. Greensboro: Morgan Reynolds Inc., 1996.

Noll, Richard. *The Aryan Christ: The Secret Life of Carl Jung*. New York: Random House, 1997.

Oates, Stephen B. *Abraham Lincoln, The Man Behind the Myth*. New York: Harper, 1984

Payne, Robert and Nikita Romanoff. *Ivan the Terrible*. New York: Thomas Crowell, 1975.

Penfield, Marc. *2001: The Penfield Collection*. Seattle: Vulcan Books, 1979.

Remnick, David. *King of the World: Muhammed Ali and the Rise of the American Hero*. New York: Random House, 1998.

Robinson, Sugar Ray, with Dave Anderson. *Sugar Ray: The Sugar Ray Robinson Story*. New York: Da Capo Press, 1994.

Rodden, Lois. *Profiles of Women: A Collection of Astrological Biographies*. Tempe: American Federation of Astrologers, 1979.

Solomon, Maynard. *Mozart: A Life*. New York: Harper Collins, 1995

Teague, Allison L. *Prince of the Fairway: The Tiger Woods Story*. Greensboro: Avisson Press, Inc., 1997.

Tenzin Gyatso, Dalai Lama XIV, and Howard C. Cutler. *The Art of Happiness, a Handbook for Living*. New York: Riverhead Books, 1998.

Van der Post, Laurens. *Jung and the Story of Our Time*. New York: Pantheon, 1975.

Webster's Ninth New Collegiate Dictionary. Springfield, MA: Merriam-Webster, 1990.

Woods, Earl. *Training a Tiger*. New York, NY: Harper Collins, 1997.

Citation for Allen Ginsberg. www.charm.net/~brooklyn/People/Allen Ginsberg.html and www.charm.net/~brooklyn/Peoms/Howl.html

Citation for Celine Dion. www.celineonline.com/bio_4.html

Citation for Jesse Ventura. www.geocities.com/Colosseum/3025/ventura.htm

Citation for Madonna. www.execpc.com/~reva/html7f.htm

Citation for Neil Armstrong. www.astronauts.org/astronauts/armstrong.htm

Citation for Timothy Leary. www.leary.com/Biography

INDEX

REACH FOR THE MOON

Llewellyn publishes hundreds of books on your favorite subjects!
To get these exciting books, including the ones on the following pages,
check your local bookstore or order them directly from Llewellyn.

Order by Phone

- Call toll-free within the U.S. and Canada, 1-800-THE MOON
- In Minnesota, call (651) 291-1970
- We accept VISA, MasterCard, and American Express

Order by Mail

- Send the full price of your order (MN residents add 7% sales tax) in U.S. funds, plus postage & handling to:

 Llewellyn Worldwide
 P.O. Box 64383, Dept. 1-56718-147-3
 St. Paul, MN 55164-0383, U.S.A.

Postage & Handling

(For the U.S., Canada, and Mexico)

- $4.00 for orders $15.00 and under
- $5.00 for orders over $15.00
- No charge for orders over $100.00

We ship UPS in the continental United States. We ship standard mail to P.O. boxes. Orders shipped to Alaska, Hawaii, the Virgin Islands, and Puerto Rico are sent by first-class mail. Orders shipped to Canada and Mexico are sent surface mail.

International orders: Airmail—add freight equal to price of each book to the total price of order, plus $5.00 for each non-book item (audio tapes, etc.).

Surface mail—Add $1.00 per item.

Allow 2 weeks for delivery on all orders.
Postage and handling rates subject to change.

Discounts

We offer a 20% discount to group leaders or agents. You must order a minimum of 5 copies of the same book to get our special quantity price.

Free Catalog

Get a free copy of our color catalog, *New Worlds of Mind and Spirit.* Subscribe for just $10.00 in the United States and Canada ($30.00 overseas, airmail). Many bookstores carry *New Worlds*—ask for it!

Visit our website at www.llewellyn.com for more information.

For readers of

Power of the Midheaven

only

FREE Natal Chart Offer

Thank you for purchasing *Power of the Midheaven*. There are a number of ways to construct a chart wheel. The easiest way, of course, is by computer, and that's why we are giving you this one-time offer of a free natal chart. This extremely accurate chart will provide you with a great deal of information about yourself. Once you receive a chart from us, *Power of the Midheaven* will provide everything you need to know to interpret your Midheaven's potential.

Also, by ordering your free chart, you will be enrolled in Llewellyn's Birthday Club! From now on, you can get any of Llewellyn's astrology reports for 25% off when you order within one month of your birthday! Just write "Birthday Club" on your order form or mention it when ordering by phone. As if that wasn't enough, we will mail you a FREE copy of our fresh new book *What Astrology Can Do for You!* Go for it!

Complete this form with your accurate birth data and mail it to us today. Enjoy your adventure in self-discovery through astrology!

Do not photocopy this form. Only this original will be accepted.

Please Print

Full Name:_____

Mailing Address:_____

City, State, Zip:_____

Birth time:_____ A.M. P.M. (please circle)

Month:_____ Day:_____ Year:_____

Birthplace (city, county, state, country):

_____

_____

Check your birth certificate for the most accurate information.

Complete and mail this form to: Llewellyn Publications, Special Chart Offer, P.O. Box 64383, 1-56718-147-3, St. Paul, MN 55164.

Allow 4–6 weeks for delivery.

Charting Your Career
The Horoscope Reveals Your Life Purpose
Stephanie Jean Clement

Clients repeatedly ask astrologers for help with career decisions. *Charting Your Career* provides a unified, elegant, and comprehensive method for analyzing a birth chart and considering the impact of current conditions on career. You will find a fresh approach and new insights, based on the author's psychological and astrological counseling practices.

This book will help you to define your own creativity, see the best path to career success and identify how your skills and life experience fit into the vocational picture. It will help you to understand why your present job is not satisfying, and what you can do to change that. It can help you see where you may have missed opportunities in the past and how to make the most of new ones as they arise. It even shows what kind of building is best for you to work in! Finally, you can see your larger spiritual mission in light of your work abilities.

1-56718-144-9, 208 pp., 7½ x 9⅛   **$12.95**

To order, call 1-800-THE MOON
Prices subject to change without notice

Dreams

Working Interactive

with Software for Journaling & Interpretation

Stephanie Jean Clement, Ph.D.,
and Terry Rosen

Dreams is the only complete and interactive system for helping you determine the unique, personal meaning of your dreams. What does it mean to dream of the house you grew up in? Why do certain people appear in your dreams again and again? How can you tell if a dream is revealing the future? Together, the book and software program provide everything necessary to effectively record and analyze whatever message your subconscious throws your way.

Absent in *Dreams* is the psychological jargon that makes many dream books so difficult. Examples of dreams illustrate the various types of dreams, and each chapter gives information about how to identify and work with dream symbols. The software program gives you the capacity to print out your dreams, incorporating the symbol definitions you select. What's more, the program will facilitate further exploration of your dreams with suggestions and questions.

With the PC-compatible Interactive Dream Software you can:
• Record your dreams, visions or waking experiences
• Get an immediate listing of your dream symbols that are included in the electronic dictionary
• Add your own new definitions to the database
• Answer questions to facilitate more in-depth exploration of your dreams

**1-56718-145-7, 240 pp., 7½ x 9⅛,
CD-ROM software program for PC format with Windows**   **$24.95**

To order, call 1-800-THE MOON
Prices subject to change without notice